The Voice of Anfield

This edition first published in 1996
by
Sport In Word Limited
Specialist Sports Publishers

ISBN: 1 874645 88 4

Sport In Word Limited
Chorley, England

ABOUT THE AUTHOR

A former journalist with XTRA time, a fortnightly newspaper devoted to Liverpool FC, Eddie Cotton is now a full time author. His first book, 'Back Where We Belong,' sold out its print run within a couple of months of being published in 1995. His second book, 'The Voice of Anfield,' is further proof of his prolific writing capabilities.

He has also been involved in local radio and TV programmes and also writes articles on a freelance basis for various football publications.

Eddie lives alone in Kensington, Liverpool, and in his spare time likes to indulge in a number of sporting activities, namely, swimming, cycling, as well as having the occasional bet on the horses.

ACKNOWLEDGEMENTS

In the writing of this book I have been assisted greatly, both in terms of interviews and help with pictures by a large number of individuals. In this respect, thanks are in order to Keith Stanton, for the loan of many of the programmes featured inside the book. Keith can be found on Anfield match-days inside the Liverpool Supporters club, on Lower Breck Road, where supporters can purchase Liverpool FC programmes, both old and new, at a reasonable price. Hope you like the advert, Keith!

Thanks are also due to the many Liverpool supporters who gave up their time to talk about their experiences following Liverpool Football Club, in this country and abroad. Also, thanks are in order to Eddie McCormack, who managed to fix my computer, after it had crashed twice during the writing of this book. Without his help I would have laid 4/6 that my fist went through the screen during those two soul destroying occasions when the computer went haywire.

Thanks as well to all my family: My mother, Pat Cotton, brothers, John, Ronnie, Terry and Stephen, as well as sisters, Patsy and Julie, who have all, in their inimitable way, helped me out at various times, in the past. In particular, I would like to thank my nephew, Kevin Sims, who kindly lent me his computer to write the book on. Incidentally, apologies for keeping you waiting for your computer, Kevin! Thanks also to Louise Gregg, who helped set up the longest and certainly most eye-opening interview I carried out, with John Swift.

I must also mention my three children, Natalie, Jade Marie and Elliot Thomas who, hopefully, will have reason to be proud of their dad, one day.

Many thanks to the staff and players of Liverpool Football Club who kindly allowed me access to the canteen at Melwood, where I carried out my interviews with the players. They generously gave up their free time to contribute to the book and I'm extremely grateful for the kind words and ample contributions they made. It's true to say that without those comments this book would have been much poorer for their absence.

Singular mention must also be made to my girlfriend, without whom this book may never have been started. Thanks, gorgeous features for all the pick-me-ups you so kindly and lovingly provided. I might not have appreciated them at the time but I sure do now!

DEDICATION

To Maria,
whose tolerance and understanding played a large part in the writing of
this book.

INTRODUCTION

When I set out to write this book in August 1996 I had a fair idea it would turn out to be an entertaining read. No book written about the exploits of Liverpool supporters could fail to be that. During the course of interviewing the fans I came across many stories concerning the exploits, both remarkable and witty, of Liverpool supporters, as they travelled the length and breadth of both Britain and Europe following their beloved team. Each and every one of those stories, turned out to be everything I expected them to be; witty, funny and remarkable. Of course, Liverpool supporters have always possessed that rare quality, namely, the ability to turn any incident into a comic situation, with their unique brand of humour. There are many instances of Scouser's legendary sense of humour inside the pages of this book. There are gems galore, such as the time when a Liverpool fan, seeking divine inspiration before the 1977 European Cup final in Rome, risked the wrath of God by vomiting at the feet of Pope Paul, as he gave his blessing in a packed Sistine Chapel. Or, the Liverpool fan, from Stockbridge Village, who decided, on a whim, to travel to Amsterdam for a pre-season game, without a penny in his pocket. Knowing the ingenuity of Scouser's you can probably guess at his means of survival. There are many such stories told in this volume and, without pre-empting anything, I know every Liverpool supporter, both old and young, will enjoy reading the accounts of their fellow supporters as they recall their adventures following Liverpool FC.

From an FA Cup tie against Worcester City, in 1959, right up to the present day, the fans describe their adventures in a witty, outrageous and entertaining style. From sleeping on barges in the middle of Amsterdam to 'bunking' into hotel bedrooms in the middle of the night. The stories they tell will certainly enlighten the more conservative minded football fans in this country. Knowing Scousers' reputation for ingenuity, it couldn't be any different, could it? Liverpool supporters, through their exploits, have always been regarded by other team's fans as a breed apart.

sense of humour and witty sarcasm have certainly played their part in distinguishing Reds' supporters from their counterparts in other parts of the country. The Liverpool players acknowledge the part the fans have played over the years in helping to inspire them with their wonderful support, both at Anfield and away from home. The extent of this partnership is there for all to see as the players wax lyrical about the contribution made by Liverpool supporters to the team's cause over the years.

It goes both ways too, as some of the fans relate their experiences of kind deeds done in their name by Liverpool players in the past. The fans involved describe the generosity of some of the players, in particular, Kenny Dalglish, for providing them with match tickets when all hope was lost. That story and many more are to be found within these pages.

During the course of this book some of the fans have managed to contribute three or four tales, while some supporters had only one story to contribute. This doesn't owe anything to favouritism. It's just that the fans concerned had further tales to tell, which I quickly realised would be of interest to the reader. In particular are the stories which Jim Gardiner recounted. As most Liverpool supporters know, Jim is a real die-hard Reds fan. This guy travels everywhere........and I mean everywhere with Liverpool Football Club. His stories of travelling to Dubai and Singapore, when only a handful of Liverpool fans made those trips, help make the book a more enlightening and enjoyable read, in my opinion.

On a more dubious note, there are plenty of tales of Liverpool fans 'running the gauntlet' as they travelled to various 'shady' cities to see their team play. The 1970's were a prime example of this period of trouble when every away ground and city Liverpool played in was a potential mine-field for trouble on the terraces and in the surrounding streets. This period of footballing history is well chronicled as Reds fans describe their adventures during that hooligan dominated decade. Visits to the likes of out which the supporters concerned will never forget, for a variety of reasons. And talking about the 1970's, no travelling Liverpool supporter at the time couldn't fail to recall that incident at Leicester railway station when hooligans set fire to the special train which had been booked to take them back to Liverpool. As a result, British Rail cancelled all special trains for Liverpool supporters after that. That particular story and many more are contained within the pages of this book. Younger Reds fans will realise the legacy which has been left them by older supporters. Many of the fans reading this will not have been born when some of the matches described were taking place. No matter, as the stories told will make the younger fans realise the extent of the support and loyalty which Liverpool Football Club have always enjoyed. If anybody has ever wondered what makes Liverpool supporters go to the lengths they do to support their team then read this book. The tales they tell will certainly open your eyes to the ingenuity, humour and sheer bravado used to follow the men in red. The anecdotes and stories which make up The Voice of Anfield, epitomise the unswerving and loyal support shown by the fans of Liverpool Football Club, over the years. As the players themselves are quick to admit: 'Liverpool fans are, quite simply, the best supporters in the world!'

THE VOICE OF ANFIELD

The Fans

OFFICIAL SOUVENIR PROGRAMME £1·50

EVERTON LIVERPOOL

FOOTBALL ASSOCIATION CHALLENGE CUP COMPETITION

 CUP FINAL

WEMBLEY STADIUM

JOHN BATES
Unemployed Scaffolder

Liverpool v Everton
1986 FA Cup Final

Four of us, Stevie, Touchy, Graham and myself left Tuebrook around 10 o'clock on Friday morning by car. We were due to meet a load of mates in Harrow on the Hill later that afternoon and we set off after stopping at an off-licence for a load of ale for the journey down to London. We arrived at 3pm and met up with the rest of the lads at the hotel. We had a bevvy and a few laughs in the bar - Liverpudlians and Evertonians together. Then we had a quick shower and change before going out for the night. We arrived in Harrow and found this big alehouse which was chock-a-block as there was a heavy metal band playing. Half of us were already bevvied, having been on the ale all day. Anyway, I bumped into a fella I knew from Huyton, who was living down there, and I had a drink with him. After a few more drinks I was bladdered and I remember jumping up onto the stage where this heavy metal band were playing. I took the microphone off the singer and asked him, 'Any chance of playing any Beatles songs?' He just looked at me as if I was fucking mad. Anyway, I kept hold of the microphone and started singing, Yellow Submarine, to all these fellas with long hair who had come to see the band. I don't know what I sounded like but I know that halfway through the song I forgot the words. Everybody in the audience must have been thinking, 'Who the fucking hell is he?' By this time, all the lads from Liverpool were screaming, 'Get the fucking hell down, will yer, John. You're gonna get us fucking killed here!' I was oblivious at this stage and remember shouting down the microphone, 'fuck them,' before carrying on with my singing.

We finally got out of the alehouse after closing time and went to a chippy. We'd missed the last train back to Harrow on the Hill by now and we were wondering how to get back to the hotel. Next thing, one of the lads spotted a black fella pulling into a garage to get petrol in one of those little Bedford vans. We all ran over and jumped into this van, saying to the fella, 'Take us to Harrow on the Hill, will yer!' The fella had no choice as there were about 14 of us crammed into the back of his van, with another three sitting on the passenger seat next to him, by now. His bottle had gone - understandably so, I suppose, but he summoned enough courage to protest, 'It's out of my way and my fish and chips are going to go cold.' One of the lads piped up, 'Don't worry, we'll have a whip-round, for you!' Nobody was about to get out of his van, anyway, and so he accepted the situation and drove off. When he realised we weren't about to mug or hurt him he was alright with us. He was a nice fella too, and we soon got talking about football. Eventually, he dropped us off right outside the hotel and we had a few more bevvies in the hotel bar before trying to find a bed for the night. I'd bunked in but luckily had found an empty room with a double bed inside. I just crashed out on top of it and fell asleep. Next thing I remember was being woken up by two of the hotel staff. I didn't know what day it was, by this time, and I was looking around, asking, 'Where the fuck am I?' I was lying in the corridor, outside the manager's office. I must have slept-walked in the middle of the night. The two hotel staff tried to throw me out but I wouldn't go and they eventually called the police. The copper turned up and asked, 'What's going on?' He must have sussed that I wasn't supposed to be there and he said, 'Come on lad, we'll lock you up for the night.' To be honest, the police weren't too bad about it, once I'd admitted not paying for the room. The sergeant told me, 'We won't charge you, we'll just give you a caution, and let you go in the morning.' To be honest, I was grateful to have a roof over my head - and so I grabbed a blanket and got my head down on the floor of the cell. They let me out about 6 o'clock in the morning and I walked back to the hotel. I was sitting on the wall outside the hotel because I couldn't get back inside the building - everywhere was locked. One of the lads finally came out and he asked, 'We put you to bed last night, what the fucking hell are you doing out here?' When I told him the story he was in bulk, laughing. He went off to tell the rest of the lads and I eventually managed to sneak back into the hotel to have a shower and change my clothes.

We went to the match then and had a bevvy in a nice alehouse near Wembley Way. After the game we came out and went back to the hotel in Harrow on the Hill. Later that night, the same two fellas who had found me in the corridor the night before spotted me in the bar. Next thing, this big black fella comes over and says, 'Drink up, will you, you're going to have to leave the premises.' I didn't want to cause any trouble, so I said, 'I'll go after I've finished my drink.' He said, 'Don't worry, you can have you're money back, instead.' By the time I'd got to the door and asked for my money back the fella said, in a cockney accent, 'You're fucking joking, aren't you? If you don't get out now, I'll throw you out.' I got a cob-on then and said, 'Well, fucking try it then.' He threatened to call the police and so I shot off, before he managed to get to the phone. The lads eventually came out and we all made our way to this alehouse around the corner. It was only a small pub but the people in there were very friend ly and they made us welcome. A big load of Chelsea fans came in then, all dressed in blue and white favours. I think they were from a public school across the road. There was no bother, or anything like that, and later on we passed this party which was going on in a basement flat. One of the lads, Touchy, has got a big lash, and he suddenly decided to get it out and wave it through this open window where the party was going on. There were unmerciful screams as the girls in the party saw this thing being swung through the window.

Later on, we were walking along the street when I suddenly saw a load of Liverpool supporters going into this house across the road. 'Come on, let's see where they're going. It might be a party,' I said. It turned out they were going into the house to watch Match of the Day. We just said, 'Any chance of coming in to watch the game,' and they said, 'Yeah, come in.' The people who lived in the house were Liverpool supporters and they made us really feel at home, handing out coffee and sandwiches as we sat in their living room watching the game. We thanked them and left around I am to make our way back. There was no way I could get into the hotel though, because, by this time, they had guards on the door. I decided to give it a miss and I slept in Graham's car all night. We set off for Liverpool at 9 o'clock on Sunday morning and I couldn't wait to get back to my own bed for a good night's sleep.

EDDIE COTTON
Author

St. Etienne v Liverpool
First leg, European Cup, Quarter Final,
March 1977

So there we were, 300 Liverpudlians standing patiently outside the offices of Crown Coaches, in St. John's Lane, one Monday evening, the last day of February, 1977. It had cost each of us £25 for the privilege of spending almost five days on a cramped coach to the south of France and back. I didn't care though, I was young, foolish and carefree in those days. I'd taken a week's holiday from my former job as a printer/compositor, I had plenty of money and high hopes that the Reds could dispose of the French giants.

To reach the quarter-finals of that season's European Cup, Liverpool had disposed of Crusaders of Belfast the previous September by a rather hefty scoreline before trouncing the Turks of Trabzsponspor at Anfield, in the next round, after losing the first leg 1-0 in Turkey. The subsequent pairing of Liverpool and St. Etienne, last year's losing European Cup finalists, was the plum draw of the round.

Armed with enough corned beef sandwiches to feed half the coach, we eventually set off from town at 7.30pm. My mate, John Gargan, started the first chant, as soon as we had turned right into Lime Street. 'We love you Liverpool, we do.........etc,' at the top of his voice. Everybody joined in, why not, we were on our way to a foreign country to watch our beloved Liverpool? By the time we hit the M62 in Broadgreen the coach was bouncing with hearty renditions of every tune from the Kop songbook. The first service station we stopped at was Burtonwood (and, now with hindsight, apologies to the people of Burtonwood). As they invariably do, things soon developed into one of those free-for-all's which Scousers seem to revel in to this day. We cleared Burtonwood services of its entire stock of sweets, chocolates, pasties, sausage rolls, coke and sandwiches. You name it, we robbed it, before quickly disposing of the evidence in the only way we could - by scoffing the lot on the coach! I felt sorry for the lone shop assistant as she valiantly tried to repel the red hordes who descended on the shop. It was a forlorn effort on her part as the flow was impossible to stop.

Meanwhile, one or two professional Scouse thieves decided to disregard the cheese & onion crisps, Mars Bars and cans of Fanta by heading for the till. While the robbers were getting their thieving hands on the pound notes, the harassed assistant was elsewhere trying to regain a box of salt & vinegar crisps which, by now, had been evenly distributed to the 50 or so members of Coach No. 4. Luckily for us, the local police must have been deployed on more urgent matters that night as they were nowhere to be seen throughout this period of pillaging.

By 2.30am most of the occupants of our coach had retired for the night. As the convoy of coaches drove through London, most of the fans were fast asleep, including myself. All except for one madman, from Netherley, who insisted on warning everybody on the coach, in a loud voice that West Ham would be waiting for us at the Blackwall tunnel. 'Nobody's going to be waiting for us, you soft bastard, it's a quarter to three in the fucking morning,' somebody shouted. This seemed to have the desired effect, as the guy finally sat down in his seat. Glancing over in his direction, I couldn't help but notice that he continued to shoot nervous glances out of the window every time the coach stopped at traffic lights.

We arrived in Dover at 5.30am and were immediately confronted by a long line of policemen, ready, willing and able to quell any disorder from travelling Scouse hooligans. They had nothing to fear because all 300 of us were half unconscious from the long journey south. Our spirits were revived somewhat on the trip over the Channel (the sea air does wonders for your constitution). Very little got robbed, largely because of the fact the shipping line had closed the duty free shop as a precaution. Can you blame them, after the slaughter of Burtonwood, a mere eight hours earlier? As a sideline, my friends, Mono, John Gargan and Billy Hignett and I decided to embark on a mission to try and find some girls to cop-off with before the ship reached Calais. After a long walk round every deck we finally managed to locate a party of Cockney schoolgirls on their way to Bordeaux on a school trip. We tried, in our own inimitable scally way to cop off with them, but, believe it or not, they were having none of it. We managed to convince ourselves that it wasn't because we were ugly, it was just that we were unlucky.

By the outskirts of Paris we had recovered from the shock of being knocked back by the schoolies and, as a result of this renewed confidence, decided to treat the good citizens of Paris to a spot of mooning. While we were busy sticking our bums out of the windows the other residents of the coach were serenading the gay city with a rousing rendition of, 'The Reds are coming up the hill, boys........!' Paris behind us, we sped south, stopping numerous times at various places - basically to use the toilet. All told, we must have stopped at least two dozen times. In the end, the driver got pissed off himself and insisted that we pee out of the windows for the rest of the journey. By this stage, serious inroads were being made into my still well-stocked sandwich box. Indeed, my mother would have been pleased as punch at the kind comments made by the fans as they chomped merrily on the last of the corned beef sandwiches.

All that day, Tuesday, we travelled south. By now, plans were being hatched as to how best to spend the forthcoming day in Lyons. We ditched plans for a fist-fight with the early morning French commuters, as none of us wanted to get arrested before the big game. Instead, a few of us decided to find somewhere to get a good wash and brush-up and a decent breakfast before prowling the avenues of Lyons in search of fun. Mono and I, would you believe, copped off with two gorgeous girls we met in Lyons' equivalent of our St. John's market. I'm telling you straight, I fell in love with my girl. Her name was Laurence Gorood, and, as we walked hand in hand (honest) through the streets, I didn't give a thought to Messrs Clemence, Smith, Jones, Keegan, or the much coveted European Cup. I was so besotted with this dark haired girl that I bought her a box of French chocolates, much to the amusement of Mono, who proceeded to take the piss for the rest of the day. To cut a long love story short, the two of us spent the morning and afternoon together, kissing and walking and kissing some more before I had to leave for the coach at 4.30pm. I was heartbroken and she looked as if she was about to pass out as we waved goodbye for the last time. I stepped on board the coach and the lads were giving me loads of stick for kissing her in front of them. It wasn't their fault, I suppose. They were just jealous guys.

But back to business, and our convoy of coaches arrived in the town of St. Etienne at 6pm, much to the curious bemusement of many thousands of French football supporters who were already crowding the streets and pavements around the ground. The place looked intimidating, with green and white flags, scarves and banners everywhere. From windows above the street, people looked down on us as we began chanting, 'Liverpool...... Liverpool,' more to keep up our own morale, than anything else. The noise as we entered the stadium was impressive, much noisier than any of us had expected. The Liverpudlians in the crowd struggled to make themselves heard above the din the French supporters were making. As the two teams entered the arena the first real surge of noise came from the Reds' fans who were congregated in one corner of the ground. 'Walk on, walk on, with hope in your hearts, and you'll never walk alone, you'll never walk alone,' the most famous Liverpool FC song was sung with feeling and passion by every Liverpudlian present. It was a case of every Liverpudlian having to sing because any noise we did make was invariably deafened by the noise of the St. Etienne fans. Our immediate objective, as visiting supporters, was to try and out-sing the popular St. Etienne end, where, believe it or not, we were actually situated. That particular objective was understandably forgotten as St. Etienne's finest suddenly came at us armed to the teeth with knives and bottles. The three or four hundred 'boys' amongst the travelling Liverpool contingent, quite admirably, stood their ground. Some guy I knew from Croxteth shouted, 'Stay!' and we all stayed to face the French hordes who were within 20 yards of us on the packed terrace. Suddenly, a huge gap appeared in the terraces as a crew of about 40 Liverpool fans (Anny Roaders, to a man) stormed down from the top of the terraces into the St. Etienne boys. All hell suddenly let loose, as the French retreated under this unexpected but lethal onslaught. The sight of victory had the effect of galvanising the main army of Liverpool fans, who suddenly marched forward with renewed vigour, attacking any French fan unfortunate enough to be standing in their path. But the fightback didn't last long as a large proportion of their home end fans, having seen their compatriots thoroughly outfoxed and beaten, suddenly decided to move en masse toward the retreating Liverpool supporters. There was nothing cowardly about our retreat. Indeed, it made good sense not to stay where we were, a mere ten yards from the goalmouth, because that was where the main body of St. Etienne boys were congregated. Luckily, for us anyway, the gendarmerie then decided to intervene in the matter. This timely intervention had the effect of saving our face and our skins.

St. Etienne scored the only goal of the game through midfielder Bathenay, thus setting up one of Anfield's greatest ever nights two weeks hence. Though disappointed at not having secured a draw in this first leg, the main concern for every Liverpudlian in the ground that night, wasn't about the goings-on on the pitch. Of more concern was how to get back to the coaches in one piece, with this gang of murderous French cut-throats about?

To be honest, things weren't so bad outside the ground. The St. Etienne supporters, happy at the result, gave us a walkover. Little groups of ten and 20 of their boys were standing on every corner, but they didn't come near to fight. We weren't to know this though, as the Liverpool contingent marched out of the ground, like an army, ready and willing to do battle. 'Scousers, stick together,' became the rallying cry as 1,000 of us made our way back to the coach-park, a half mile away. Once back at the coach-park things cooled down somewhat, with conversations taking place between both sets of fans. 'Oo eez ze 'ardest team in England?' was one question the St. Etienne hooligans were keen to have answered. Full of bravado, having made it safely back to the coach-park, we proceeded to lie through our collective teeth, informing them that Liverpool had one of the hardest mobs in Britain. Just before we climbed on board the coach we did our bit for French/Anglo relations by swapping our scarves, banners and badges with their fans. I managed to secure one of those infamous green afro wigs (which I've still got, to this day). Nothing much of note happened on the long journey home. I was glad of that anyway, because it gave the opportunity of some much needed sleep, albeit in cramped and sweaty conditions on the coach. Nevertheless, of that trip will always bring back happy memories for me.

● ● ● ● ● ● ● ● ● ● ● ● ● ● ● ● ●

JOHN BATES
Unemployed Scaffolder

Liverpool v Nottingham Forest
League Cup Final, Wembley,
March 1978

It was around 10am on the day of the match and Wembley was awash with Liverpudlians. For some reason the Nottingham Forest supporters hadn't arrived and so the Scousers had the place to themselves, more or less. The bulk of the crowd hanging around Wembley were young scallywags. But the general atmosphere was well-behaved with fellas playing football (200 hundred a side!) on the car-park. I'd been on the ale the night before and was paying the consequences for it. It didn't help that I'd had nothing to eat since Friday dinner-time. Having travelled overnight by train to London, still without anything to eat, I began to feel sick. I was standing on the steps of Wembley Way, balking my guts up when the first Nottingham Forest coach pulled into the car-park, festooned with scarves and banners all over the windows. The Forest fans got off their coach singing and waving these big flags and marching toward where the vast majority of Liverpool supporters were gathered. By this time, the scallys, and there were hundreds of them, had become aware of what was happening. Suddenly, Liverpudlians seemed to come from every direction; from the front, back and sides, all closing in on these 50 or so Forest fans. Honestly, it was like that film about the Cossacks, Taras Bulba. The Liverpudlians surrounded both the coach and their fans. It was weird the way it happened because, at first, everybody was walking slow. Then, the pace picked up a little, but, at the same time, nobody said anything. Nobody talked or shouted, they just kept on walking toward these lone Forest fans. When the Liverpool supporters got to within 100 yards of their rivals, they suddenly started jogging in unison. The Forest supporters had stopped singing and waving their flags by now. I think they realised there was going to be trouble, because they began to hesitate a little. They started looking around for help but all they could see was a vast army of Liverpool scallies surrounding them, on all four sides.

Somebody shouted, 'Liverpool,' and that was it - the scallies charged into them. There was murder. One big Forest fan, he must have been about 6ft 6in, was leaning against the coach, lashing out at everybody who came near him. Next thing, one fella hit him on the head with a rolled up Echo and he went down. I was surprised he went down so easily but realised there must have been something inside the paper - an iron bar, or something like that. Next thing, the coach driver panicked and suddenly drove off like a lunatic, scattering fans all over the place. He must have been doing about 60 miles per hour out of Wembley. Only about half of their fans were on the coach, the rest were getting picked off, one by one, by the scallies. There was a bit of trouble at around 2.30pm when hundreds of their fans came round to the Liverpool end of the ground, looking for trouble. There was a lot of cans and bottles thrown but then it calmed down after police reinforcements arrived.

•••••••••••••••••

STEVE GARNER
Clothes Shop Owner

Liverpool v Everton
FA Cup Semi-Final, Old Trafford,
March 1971

In those days I had my own mobile greengrocery business, selling fruit and vegetables from a van, in Netherley. Because of this I couldn't get to many away matches but I always managed to get to Anfield for the home games. You see, my brother-in-law would turn up on his motor-bike around 2 pm to take over from me. I would then ride the bike and park it outside the ground before going to watch the match from the Anfield Road End. I was a season ticket holder in that part of the ground for many years.

For this particular match, I'd hired a car - one of those Ford Capri's - and the only other lads who were interested in going to the game turned out to be three brothers, all Evertonians. Dave, Sid and Danny Rice who were mad Evertonians, at that time. The four of us set off early for the game and, anticipating lengthy traffic jams into Manchester, we decided to take an entirely different route from everybody else. This involved dri

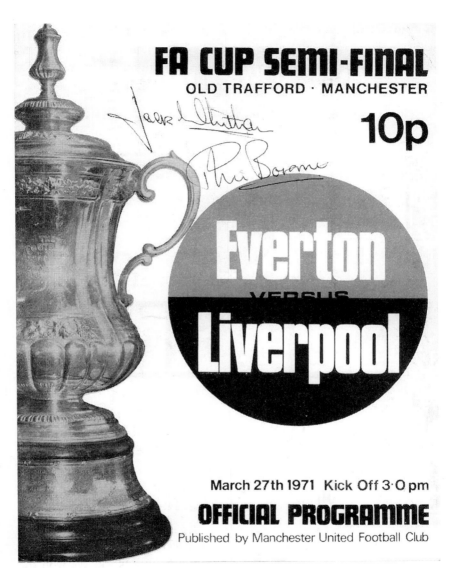

FA CUP SEMI-FINAL

OLD TRAFFORD · MANCHESTER

10p

Everton

VERSUS

Liverpool

March 27th 1971 Kick Off 3·0 pm

OFFICIAL PROGRAMME

Published by Manchester United Football Club

ving through Warrington, Lymm and Altrincham before hitting Manchester from the other side of town. Normally, you could do the trip in about 45 minutes but this day it took us two and a half hours because the traffic was so heavy. At one stage we were stuck underneath the

29

motorway and you could see all the traffic above, cars, coaches, buses, which were all at a complete standstill. Liverpool and Everton fans, obviously bored with waiting, were playing football on the hard shoulder of the motorway. This was about 12.30 pm - two and a half hours before kick-off.

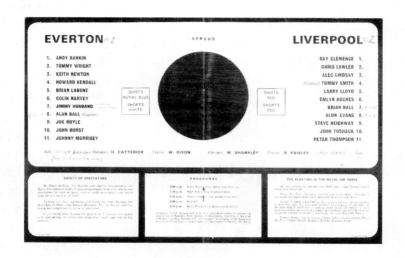

We eventually arrived at Old Trafford and managed to park the car near to the ground with about 20 minutes to spare. I stood on the Stretford End and afterwards I used to say to people that I'd stood on the Stretford End at Old Trafford and shouted for Liverpool. The three Evertonian brothers went to the other side of the ground to stand at the Scoreboard end.

That part of the ground didn't look as packed as where we were. You couldn't move in the Stretford End - it was chock-a-block. We won the game 2-1 and in the car on the journey home the two youngest Rice brothers never stopped crying. I wanted to celebrate but had to hold back the cheers for their sakes.

A couple of years later, Danny Rice, who was a good footballer, went to Melwood, Liverpool's training ground, with his mate Billy McClure, who was on Liverpool's books at the time. Danny was standing on the touchline, ready to watch the game which his mate was playing in, when Liverpool found themselves a man short. Billy said to one of the coaches, 'My mate can play a bit, you know.' The upshot of it was Danny played the full 90 minutes in this practice game. He must have impressed the coaches because they invited him back the following week. So, Danny turned up seven days later, only to find that there was a power cut at Melwood, with the result that the game got abandoned. You won't believe this, but the same thing happened the following week. By the third week, Danny, being a die-hard Evertonian, lost interest and didn't turn up for his trial. Meanwhile, his mate, Billy McClure, continued to impress the Liverpool coaches, so much so that he eventually got a few games in the Reserves. Eventually, he left the club and emigrated to New Zealand, where he played for Auckland. He made such an impression there, that the New Zealand FA eventually asked him to take out citizenship in order to allow him to play for the New Zealand national side. Billy, who used to play football with us on a Sunday afternoon on Childwall Valley High School playing fields, got to play in the World Cup finals. It was unreal watching the games on the telly and seeing him playing against all these superstars. I'd say, to anybody who would listen, 'I used to play football with him, years ago, you know!'

BOBBY YOUDS
Retired Silo Operator

Liverpool v Leeds Utd
FA Cup Final, Wembley,
May 1965

It cost me and my mate, four guineas each on a specially chartered train from Lime Street. For that price we got breakfast and dinner on the journey down to London and a four course meal on the way home. My ticket to get in the ground cost 7/6p, (about 32p in today's money). I'll always remember being nervous because you had to send the money and relevant voucher by post to Anfield. I was scared that my envelope would get lost in the system, somewhere. But it didn't and my ticket arrived a few days before the game. I was over the moon because it was Liverpool's first trip to Wembley since 1950, when we'd lost 2-0 to Arsenal. I was too young to go to that final but I'll always remember my dad hoisting me onto his shoulders on St. George's plateau to see the team come home on Sunday afternoon. Those old news-reel films, which they used to show - you can actually see my dad and me on it. I was just a kid at the time but looking at that film it strikes me that not many fans wore colours in those days. They all had collar and ties on. You might get one or two wearing old fashioned red and white striped scarves, or big bobble hats, but, in the main, nobody really wore favours, not like they do nowadays, anyway.

But, on the morning of the 1965 Cup Final, the Daily Express tipped Liverpool to win by 2-1 and we cut this headline out of the paper and stuck it on the window of our carriage as the train left Lime Street. We had our meal, which was soup, followed by a roast dinner and then a sweet; followed by cheese and biscuits and coffee. We got the ale out then. I had a bottle of scotch and my mate had a bottle of rum. So, by the time we arrived at Wembley we were all merry. Outside the ground, I've never seen so many Liverpudlians. They seemed to outnumber the Leeds supporters, three to one. The club had only received 15,000 tickets but there must have been, at least, 30,000 Reds outside Wembley that day. Hundreds must have bunked in, because they were all over the ground, not just in the Liverpool end. I don't think Wembley had seen anything like it before. And the noise they made inside the ground was unbelievable - it was just like standing on the Kop, at Anfield - it was that noisy. Of course, we won the game 2-1 and after seeing the team parade the cup round Wembley we caught the train home. On the way back, the whole train was absolutely bouncing with supporters singing and dancing - it was brilliant. The ale was flowing and everybody was celebrating the fact we'd won the cup for the first time.

LIVERPOOL F.C. 1964 - 1965

[Picture by courtesy of Liverpool Daily Post & Echo Ltd.

Back Row (*left to right*) : G. MILNE, G. BYRNE, T. LAWRENCE, C. LAWLER, R. YEATS (*Captain*) and W. STEVENSON
Front Row (*left to right*) : I. CALLAGHAN, R. HUNT, I. ST. JOHN, T. SMITH and P. THOMPSON

My mate and I decided that we'd have a quiet drink in town and then head to our local in Farnworth Street in Kensington. But the best was yet to come, because when the train pulled into Lime Street later that night there was an almighty roar coming from the station concourse. We looked out of the window of our carriage to see what was going on. We couldn't believe the sight we witnessed. There were thousands of people crowding the station, all waiting to greet the Liverpool supporters as they arrived back home. This big fella got everybody on our train together, before we marched down the platform, singing, 'We've won the cup, we've won the cup, eey aye adio, we've won the cup!' Next thing, everybody started cheering and clapping us. We made it onto the station concourse and then everybody started doing the conga - thousands of us. It was an unbelievable sight. We snaked our way out of Lime Street station and up London Road - thousands of us, doing the conga and singing our heads off. The alehouses all over town were packed with Liverpudlians celebrating the fact we'd finally won the FA Cup.

● ● ● ● ● ● ● ● ● ● ● ● ● ● ● ● ●

DAVID THOMPSON
Retired Dockworker

Worcester City v Liverpool
FA Cup 3rd Round,
January 1959

There was never any trouble in our day. When we played away from home there were always thousands of Liverpudlians travelling to watch the team play. Many of the away grounds in those days were in easy reach. You had the likes of Preston, Blackburn, Burnley, Bolton and the two Manchester clubs in the First Division, so, we didn't have too far to travel. In those days the away supporters would mingle freely with the home supporters. But, with so many of our fans travelling away from home, you would find they would automatically stick together in one part of the ground. The Liverpudlians always made lots of noise too. Manchester

City's ground was a good example of what I'm talking about because our supporters would congregate on one side of the open terracing with their rattles and scarves. The home supporters would try and out-sing us but more often than not, we were able to out-shout them. Don't forget, in those days Maine Road could hold around 60,000, and that size crowd can make a lot of noise - and they did too. But, we usually held our own when it came to cheering on the team. There was rarely any trouble at the away games. The Liverpudlians would go into the local pubs and clubs before the game to have a drink and a laugh with some of the home supporters. The only time I remember any trouble was at Old Trafford in the early sixties. Our kid and I were standing in the old Scoreboard end of the ground watching the game. I can't remember the score but I recall our kid, Franny, shouting for Liverpool while the game was going on. Next thing, this big Irish fella standing behind us, shouted, 'If I hear any of you Scousers shouting again, I'll hit you one!' Our kid, who was only little compared to this big Irish fella, turned round to him, and said, 'Who are you fuckin' talking to, you dopey looking bastard?' before hitting him right on the jaw. I've never seen anything like it. This big Irish fella just went down like a bag of shite. But apart from that, I never saw any trouble at away games involving Liverpool supporters.

But going back to this particular game, Liverpool had been drawn to play Worcester City in the third round of the FA Cup. None of us had ever heard of them. We all thought - 'Aye, aye, this should be an easy passage into the next round.' Anyway, we managed to get tickets for the game. The capacity of their ground was 15,000 and I think Liverpool received about 1,500 tickets. Our kid and I booked our tickets for the special train from Lime Street for the game on the following Saturday. We left Lime Street about 10 o'clock that morning - a trainload of 500 Liverpudlians. But, in those days, you couldn't walk through the train like you can nowadays. It was all single carriages, with a door on either side of the carriage. If you wanted to go the toilet you literally had to pee out of the window. We arrived in Worcester about 1 pm with all the out of the windows of the train, singing and shouting as we pulled into the station. As we all got off the train and headed for the gate we spotted a big line of policemen and railway guards standing at the end of the platform, all shouting, 'Alright lads, you may as well turn back - the game is off.' We couldn't believe it and so about 50 of us decided to head for the ground to see for ourselves. We got into the ground through an open gate and stood on the pitch. To be honest, it didn't look too bad - certainly playable, in my opinion. If I remember rightly, there wasn't much grass on the pitch and it was terribly muddy, but I've seen games played on worse pitches than that one. But the referee had already made his decision and so we made our way back to the station to catch the train, which left an hour or so later.

The match was finally played on the following Wednesday afternoon. I was working on the docks at the time and couldn't get time off work, so had to miss the game. My brother Franny went by car and managed to break his arm when he slipped in the snow as he came out of the ground after the match, which we lost 2-1. I'll always remember the Evertonians, for weeks later ribbing us about that game. Liverpudlians from that era would probably class it as one of the worst defeats in the club's history.

● ● ● ● ● ● ● ● ● ● ● ● ● ● ● ● ●

DENNIS THOMPSON
Barber

Blackpool v Liverpool
Division One game, mid-sixties

We had been to a game at Bloomfield Road and afterwards decided to make a night of it in Blackpool. The ex-heavyweight boxer, Brian London, had a club called the 007 and after we'd had a few bevvies we all went up to his club. The door-men wouldn't let us in at first but eventu ally we managed to talk our way into the place by saying, 'Come on, Brian, we used to watch you all the time, at the Stadium.' Eventually Brian said, 'Oh come on then, but no fucking trouble, okay, Scouse!' Once we were inside we had a great time - having a few drinks and a laugh. There were loads of Liverpudlians in there who had decided to stay in Blackpool for the night. Our Franny was getting on really well with this girl, sitting with his arm around her and buying her drinks. Suddenly, Brian London himself came over and in this deep voice, said, 'Hey, Scouse, that's my fuckin' horse you're trying to ride!' Our kid turned round and said, jokingly, 'Fuck off Brian, will yer, or I'll break your fuckin' jaw!'

For the life of me, I don't know how we got home in one piece that night. There were five of us in this gold Capri, Franny, Billy Hargreaves, Joe Smith, Frank and myself. We were all rotten drunk - me included, and I was driving! I remember, we flew over this hump-backed bridge, doing about 90 miles an hour. All the lads in the back were shouting, 'Slow down, will yer, you crazy bastard!' What made it worse, if you like, was that I was in bulk laughing as they were screaming the odds at me. Anyway, we made it safely back to Liverpool in the early hours of Sunday morning - though, for the life of me, I don't know how.

● ● ● ● ● ● ● ● ● ● ● ● ● ● ● ● ●

PETER KELLY
Cable Northwest Salesman

Liverpool v Borussia Moenchen Gladbach,
European Cup Final,
Rome, 1977

A gang of us from Breck Road left Wembley straight after the FA Cup final against Manchester United. We headed straight back to Liverpool and managed to catch last orders in the George pub on the corner of Walton Breck Road while most Liverpool supporters were probably still on the M6. We were all pig-sick after losing the cup final but after a few bevvies in the alehouse we began to look forward to Wednesday night's game in Rome. After a good night's sleep on Saturday night everybody was ready with a clean set of clothes and bags of sandwiches and ale for the long train journey to Italy. The first special train was leaving Lime Street on Sunday afternoon and all the lads from Breck Road, me included, were all on it.

When we arrived at Lime Street I was struck by the organisation, which was impressive. All the supporters were in orderly queues with their bags of sarney's and cans of ale held to their sides. Gail, my future wife, was on the trip with me and we soon settled down in one of the carriages. The journey down south was pretty quiet, apart from when the train went through a station; then the scallies would poke their heads out of the windows and shout abuse at people standing on the platform. It was just harmless fun, really - something to relieve the boredom of the journey, for them. The train finally stopped at Folkestone and all the Liverpool supporters got off the train to stretch their legs before boarding the boat to Ostend. The kids on the train started going on the mooch in Folkestone station and before you knew it were coming out with boxes of crisps, sweets and chocolate and sharing them out as they stood on the platform. The boat going over to Belgium was just the same. I suppose all the robbing which went on was part and parcel of going to see Liverpool, in those days. We eventually disembarked from the boat and got on the train which was waiting for us in Ostend. By this stage, people's personal hygiene began to suffer as we travelled through Switzerland and Germany on the second day. Empty cans of ale were being thrown out of the windows - people were playing cards or reading two day old newspapers. We were lucky because there were three carriages at the front which were separated from the rest of the train and we'd managed to secure one of these carriages. This enabled us to get to the toilet to have a wash and shave in relative comfort. From what I heard later, the toilets down the other end of the train were disgusting. I believe the flush wasn't working on most of them and people had to use them regardless - uurgh!

As for sleeping arrangements, well, we would take turns to sleep on the luggage rack above the seats. It wasn't very comfortable but we made the best of it. We travelled through some lovely countryside, especially in Switzerland. Looking at the mountains and the scenery itself took our minds off the journey which was becoming really boring by now. The only respite was when the train stopped, which it did now and again, and the 40 thieves would be scavenging in the buffet and shops before climbing back on board the train with the stolen goods. We finally hit Turin, in northern Italy, and it was noticeable the number of beggars in the street. We could see them from the train, there were loads of them, all dressed in ragged clothes. All the scallies on the train were shouting, 'Go and get a wash, you scruffy bastards!' That made me laugh because they weren't exactly smelling of roses themselves at this stage of the journey.

We finally arrived in Rome at 6 o'clock on Wednesday morning and Gail, myself and a few others all went to the Europa hotel in the centre of Rome, where we knew some friends of ours were staying. We managed to bunk into one of the rooms, where we got a wash and change of clothes. We then went sightseeing around the eternal city for the rest of the day. We went to see the Coliseum which was like a bin-yard - it was really scruffy. By this time, there were a lot of Scousers lying around in various places, looking the worse for wear. You knew they were from Liverpool because they all wore Flemings jeans rolled up to their knees, airware boots and had silly red hats on. We didn't see any Germans, at all. I don't think they turned up till about 6.30 - an hour before the game kicked off. But, everywhere you went you bumped into fellas that you knew. All the Liverpool supporters were having a drink, sunbathing in the fountains or trying to chat up the local women - without much success,

Liverpool supporters, all rotten drunk, doing the conga with about 40 young Italian kids, while singing, 'Oh Joey, Joey - Joey, Joey, Joey, Joey, Joey Jones,' in the Vatican. Every time the kids got the song right, the Scousers would throw them some coins. We went to St. Peter's square around 1.30 pm. Gail and I bumped into a friend of mine, Jughead, who was from Childwall. We called him Jughead because he had terrible ears, this fella. Anyway, the three of us were sitting in the Cathedral and Pope Paul came out, blessing everybody. He walked past us, and as soon as he did Gail grabbed my arm and said, 'Peter, I'm sorry, but I'm going to be sick!' Next thing, she threw up all over the bench in front, while the Pope was administering the blessings, not two feet away from us. He must have thought, 'Fuckin' hell, we've got the anti-christ in here today!' Suddenly, two penguins, or nuns, I should say, ran up the aisle, grabbed Gail by the arm and took her away. There was nothing we could do and so, after the Pope had finished blessing the congregation, Jughead and I headed for a nearby bar and had a few drinks. Gail joined us a couple of hours later after the nuns had finally let her go.

We left for the match itself then and it was great. There were Liverpudlians everywhere. We started seeing a few Germans then, but they seemed to be keeping a low profile. Then again, who could blame them, because there were at least 26,000 Scousers around the ground that night. It was all good humoured, though, with not a hint of trouble. The match itself was brilliant and winning the European Cup was an unbelievable experience - the best feeling I've ever had following Liverpool. After the game we found everywhere closed. We were all desperate for a drink to celebrate but all the bars and shops were shut. The only part of the city which was open was in the Lazio area of Rome, but we'd been warned not to go down there, in case of trouble with their fans. So we decided to head back to the railway station, hoping to catch the first special train back to Liverpool, which left at 12.30am. We got on the train, found an empty carriage and settled back, thinking, 'This is great, an empty train to ourselves.' Next thing, thousands of Liverpool suddenly converged on the platform, all desperate to get on this first train home. The train itself was designed to carry around 2,000 passengers but, I'm telling you, there must have been 5,000 fans, at least, on this train. It was mayhem. People were sitting on each other's knees - on the floor - on the luggage racks. It was crazy. When the train finally pulled out of Rome station there were fellas climbing through windows, trying to get on. It was like the Titanic. But amazingly enough, things weren't so bad for the first five hours or so of the journey, because everybody was finishing off what ale they had left. But after everybody had sobered up, it became apparent that things weren't exactly pleasant. Don't forget, there were fellas who hadn't been washed or hadn't changed their clothes for five days, by now. As you can imagine, the stink was terrible. People were farting, burping and generally smelling something rotten. It was like the black hole of Calcutta. It got so bad that fellas were throwing their dirty clothes out of the window. Some of them were just peeling their socks off and throwing them at innocent by-standers on railway stations as the train passed by. The train stopped now and again, but every time it did there was an army of armed guards waiting for us on the platform. The young scallies still managed to grab a handful of food and drink, though, - and obviously, they never thought to pay for it. We got back into Lime Street around 5 o'clock on Friday afternoon. Some of the lads went straight up to Anfield for Tommy Smith's testimonial game. I didn't bother because all I wanted was a hot shower, something to eat and a good night's sleep after all that travelling.

PETER KELLY
Cable Northwest Salesman

Liverpool v West Ham United
League Cup Final, 1981

We had seven cars and two vans which went from the Willowbank pub in Breck Road. One of the vans kept breaking down, though. In the end, we sent one of the kids who was in the van with us to siphon some petrol from a works van, which was parked up next to us in Watford Gap services. We'd arranged to meet in one of the side streets by Wembley Central. There must have been about 60 of us, all from Breck Road, who made our way to the match. We always used to stay a little bit separate from the rest of the Liverpool mob, because we would probably end up fighting with some of them. Breck Road had a reputation in those days and half the time we would be fighting with other gangs from other parts of the city, both at Anfield and at away grounds. So, for that reason, the lads from Breck Road always stayed apart from everybody else. At home games, there would normally be about 120 of us in the Anfield Road end. We would fight with either the away supporters or with other mobs from either Walton, Childwall or Earle Road. Even away from football, there was trouble. If we went to town for a drink, we would always go mob-handed. There were certain pubs in town that we drank in and for that reason no other mobs would visit. And for the same reasons, there were pubs that we didn't bother going in because we knew there would be trouble if we did.

At this West Ham game, there was a little bit of trouble on the way to the ground but nothing too heavy. But afterwards there was murder all the way back to Wembley Central. It started off when the main Liverpool crew got chased outside Wembley by about 2,000 cockneys. Our mob,

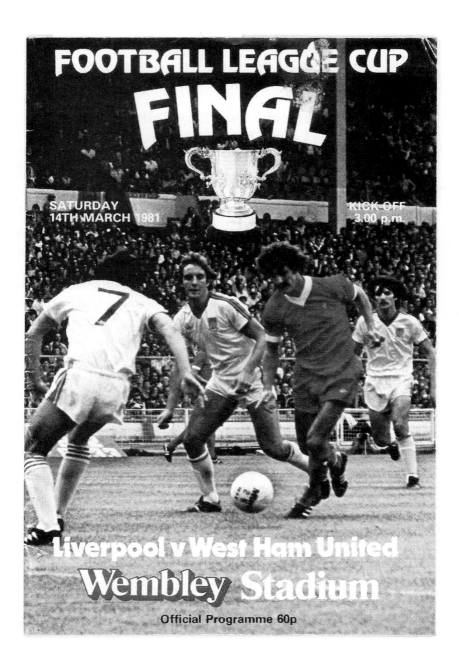

from Breck Road, weren't involved at this stage but we began walking back in the general direction of where our cars and vans were parked. We were expecting trouble to come but nothing like what occurred minutes later. The police, who had been escorting the Liverpool supporters back to Wembley Central suddenly shit themselves as this huge mob from West Ham converged on the Liverpool contingent. The coppers were just standing in the middle of the High Street, holding their truncheons, and looking totally petrified as the fighting was going on all around them. It was a scary situation to be in because West Ham were well tooled up and

Back Row (left to right): Avi Cohen, Phil Neal, Ray Clemence, Steve Ogrizovic, Alan Hansen, Colin Irwin, Ian Rush. Centre: Joe Fagan (Asst. Manager), Richard Money, David Fairclough, Ray Kennedy, David Johnson, Graeme Souness, Alan Kennedy, Ronnie Moran (Coach). Front Row: Jimmy Case, Steve Heighway, Kenny Dalglish, Bob Paisley (Manager), Phil Thompson (Captain), Terry McDermott, Sammy Lee.

most of their mob looked like big, hairy grocks. You literally had to fight your way past people, just to save yourself from being caught by their mob. Our mob from Breck Road managed to fight our way through but then we got split up. There were about 20 of us down one sidestreet and the rest were in another street. I was one of the 20 who were caught unawares by the surge of people, all struggling to escape the clutches of the cockneys. I'll always remember what happened next. There was a great roar from this mob of 2,000 and then they attacked us. It put the fear of God up me, I can tell you. We had a 20 yard start on them but in the process of trying to push past people I fell over. Next thing, this big bone-head lurched toward me and started kicking me. The next few moments were some of the worst I've ever encountered in my whole life. I got such a hiding, it was unbelievable. I had an ear-ring in one ear - that got ripped out, along with half of my ear. I had a cross and chain - this got pulled off me, near strangling me in the process. By this stage, I was rolled up into a ball but the kicking continued for what seemed an eternity. In the end, I managed to roll under a car to escape the flying boots which were still raining in on me. They left me then and I managed to get up off the floor, though I could hardly walk. I somehow managed to make it back to the pick-up point, only to find three of the cars and one of the vans on fire. We all piled into the one remaining van and after it had all died down, drove back to Liverpool, nursing our bruises.

●●●●●●●●●●●●●●●●

PETER KELLY
Cable Northwest Salesman

Leicester City v Liverpool
Division One game, 1970's

It was that infamous day when the mail train was set on fire by Liverpool supporters at Leicester station. All the lads that I knew from Breck Road were in their mid-twenties by now and so we used to get the ordinary train to most away games. All the damage was done by young scallies, from Liverpool. In all, there were about 25 of us from Breck Road who attended this particular game. As always, we stayed apart from the main Liverpool mob. We preferred to do our own scallying, on the quiet. After the game we took off straight away. We saw a few shops getting done in by the main Liverpool mob, but we kept away from that. We were walking along, looking for the Leicester crew. We ended up in this park where we suddenly spotted a gang of Paki skinheads walking toward the spot where we were hiding in wait. There was a crew from Allerton, also lying in wait for the Leicester skins on the other side of this big hedge. There were two brothers, called Thompson, who were with us. These two were absolute crazy bastards and completely fearless! This mob of Paki's were coming toward this big hedge, and we're behind it, waiting with bricks and bottles. I'll always remember, one of their mob had a turban on and next thing, a hand went through the hedge and this fella with the turban on got dragged into the bush by one of the Thompson brothers. The fella got absolutely battered. All our mob ran out then to confront the Leicester crew. We legged them as far as the park gates and then lost them in the crowd. There were loads of police about by this time and so we carefully made our way back to the station without drawing any attention to ourselves.

By the time we arrived back at the station there must have been at least 2,000 Liverpudlians hanging around. There were police everywhere trying to keep order, because Leicester's main crew had suddenly arrived outside the station, ready to fight with the Liverpool mob. A couple of enterprising Scousers decided to take advantage of the warring situation by opening one or two mail-bags which were lying on the platform ready to be deposited onto a waiting mail-train. One of the Scousers, a dipper from Croxteth, opened an envelope which contained a load of used bank-notes, addressed to the Bank of England, in London. There must have been about 300 quid in there. 'There's money in the mail-bags,' became the cry as the scallies became vultures - scattering letters, parcels and such like all over the platform, in anticipation of finding more money. In the end, they carried about 20 mail-bags onto the special train and began ripping them open, there and then. Five minutes later, the carriages were full of papers, boxes, catalogue stuff - everything! One of the lads to secure a pair of size twelve platform boots, which were all the rage, at the time. We were laughing, because this lad wore size ten shoes, and what's more, he had funny feet - one of them was bent. He threw the shoes he had on out of the window and he was sitting there in the carriage, wearing these stupid platform boots, with a big smile on his face. The police finally got onto the train and you should have seen the look on their faces. They were Liverpool coppers who had travelled down to the game to keep an eye on the local scallies. One of them was called Blackbeard - older Liverpool fans would probably remember this particular copper. Anyway, the first words out of his mouth were, 'What the fucking hell's happened here?' He used to carry ollies inside his glove and if he hit you with them you would know about it. Anyway, he started dragging fellas out of their seats and demanding to know, 'Who fucking did this, you robbing bastards?' The Liverpool coppers then went to war on the scallies, hitting anybody, whether they were in their seats or getting onto the train. And that's the main reason why the train got set on fire. Our mob, from Breck Road, had moved to the front two carriages, by this stage, because Blackbeard and the other coppers were battering everybody with their batons. The young scallies suddenly decided to set fire to the bottom of the train. They had a box which was full of paper which they set alight. Pretty soon, one of the carriages was fully ablaze. The train had left Leicester station, by now, and was doing about 80 miles an hour. It was like something out of a John Wayne western, with fellas throwing papers and boxes out of the window of this fast moving train, while up ahead, two of the carriages were fully alight. I half expected a posse of Indians, led by Crazy Horse to come charging over the hill, toward us, at any moment. It was that sort of movie.

When we finally arrived at Lime Street around 8pm there was a reception committee waiting for us at the end of the platform. There must have been about 200 coppers, all waiting to pounce. Everybody knew to keep quiet because if you opened your mouth the coppers would have fucking battered and then nicked you. But there is always one soft tard, isn't there? This fella, called 'Mad Peter', who was from Netherley, suddenly shouted, at the top of his voice, 'Let's fuck the coppers!' That was it then, they fucking battered him before lashing him into a waiting police van. Nobody opened their mouths as the police began searching everybody from the train. Luckily, most of the junk that had been found in the mail-bags had been thrown out of the windows, before we got back into Liverpool. Eventually, the coppers let us all go, without anybody getting a pull. British Rail decided not to put any more special trains on for football matches, involving Liverpool or Everton, after that.

• • • • • • • • • • • • • • • • •

PETER KELLY
Cable Northwest Salesman

Sheffield United v Liverpool
Division One game, 1972

One of the funniest away trips was the day Liverpool played Sheffield United at Bramall Lane, around Christmas time in the mid 1970's. The day had started with a fight, after a mob from the 'Annie' had tried, unsuccessfully, to take Sheffield United's end of the ground, and had ended in the full scale pillaging of Uttoxeter town centre, later that night. There was a gang of about 200 of us who had left early for Sheffield on the ordinary train, that morning. As we left the station, we were walking into the heart of the town centre when one of the lads spotted a Burtons shop. Some of the young kids who were with us darted into this shop and started robbing the money from the till. Next thing, these dummies which were in the window of the shop started moving. All of a sudden, these kids were running out of the shop with these seven foot dummies, dressed in suits. Pretty soon, half of Liverpool's mob were wearing these expensive suit jackets, which looked a bit out of place alongside their normal attire of Flemings jeans and heavy airware boots. We went to the

match then and instead of going into the away end of the ground, a mob of about 200 or so decided to try and take their 'end.' Whoever's idea it was to go into their end of the ground must have been fucking mental because we got battered as soon as we walked onto the terraces. We survived that by climbing over the fence at the front and then walking back along the perimeter, to where the main Liverpool contingent were gathered. After the match we all made our way back to the railway station. For some reason, we all jumped on the special train instead of waiting for the ordinary service train. I think it was because, being so near to Christmas, we all wanted to get back for a bevvy, in Liverpool.

For some reason, the 'special' had taken the East Midlands route, for the return journey. The young scallies, probably out of boredom, had been forever pulling the cord, which stops the train automatically. Because of this, the train must have stopped about seven or eight times before eventually grinding to a halt on a bridge opposite Uttoxeter racecourse. It had broken down completely on account of the cord being pulled so many times. Looking out of the windows of the train you could see the stands and home straight of the racecourse on your left and, on your right, this little sleepy village. The scallies were getting restless by now, and one or two were wondering aloud if there were any shops to rob around here?' One or two jumped off the train and started walking down this steep embankment. At first it was just a trickle, and then a stream, and then a torrent, as all hands jumped off the train and started walking toward this little sleepy village. The sight of 2,000 Scousers walking down this narrow, country lane, in the middle of the night, must have looked strange to any passer-by, but that's the way it was. The village itself had two pubs, one on either side of the High Street. In between was a jewellers, with no shutters on the windows, a post office and a butchers shop. As you can imagine, the jewellers window got put in, straightaway. They were grabbing rings, bracelets, the lot. I've never seen so many hands reaching into a shop window. In the end, they just peeled up the window and took everything. The manager of the alehouse we were in was made

Score Check

	HT	FT

Red Indicator

A Luton v Sheffield Wed.

B Arsenal v Norwich

C Coventry v West Brom.

D Crystal Pal. v Southampton

E Derby v Manchester United

F Everton v Birmingham

G Ipswich v Chelsea

H Leeds v Newcastle

I Manchester City v Stoke

J West Ham v Tottenham

K Wolves v Leicester

L Aston Villa v Nottm. Forest

M Blackpool v Burnley

N Bristol City v Cardiff

White Indicator

A Newcastle Res. v Utd. Res.

B Carlisle v Preston

C Fulham v Millwall

D Hull v Middlesbrough

E Oxford v Brighton

F Portsmouth v Swindon

G Q.P.R. v Orient

H Sunderland v Huddersfield

I Blackburn v Chesterfield

J Grimsby v Scunthorpe

K Halifax v Rotherham

L Barnsley v Mansfield

M Doncaster v Lincoln

N Hereford v Southport

Sheffield United ☐

1   Tom McALISTER
2   Len BADGER
3   Ted HEMSLEY
4   John FLYNN
5   Eddie COLQUHOUN
6   Trevor HOCKEY
7   Alan WOODWARD
8   Geoff SALMONS
9   Bill DEARDEN
10 Tony CURRIE
11 Stewart SCULLION
12

Liverpool ☐

1   Ray CLEMENCE
2   Chris LAWLER
3   Alex LINDSAY
4   Phil THOMPSON
5   Larry LLOYD
6   Emlyn HUGHES
7   Kevin KEEGAN
8   Peter CORMACK
9   Steve HEIGHWAY
10 Phil BOERSMA
11 Ian CALLAGHAN
12

Referee: P. PARTRIDGE (Middlesbrough)
Linesmen:
Red Flag, C. C. BROOKES (Sutton-in-Ashfield)
Orange Flag, N. HILTON (Oldham)

Today's referee, **PAT PARTRIDGE**, went to Japan last summer to referee and lecture. He has refereed League Cup and F.A. Cup semi-finals and run the line at Wembley. He began refereeing in 1953. On full list 1967-68. Put on F.I.F.A. panel for last season. He is a technical electrical representative.

up because the place was absolutely chock-a-block after we'd arrived. 'Five pints of lager, two whiskies and two packets of crisps, please love!' somebody would order. The barmaid would go into the back for the crisps and while her back was turned, the ale would be whisked to somebody else. 'Who ordered two whiskies and five lagers?' she asked on her return to the bar. I don't think anybody paid for a drink, in that alehouse, that night. While we were in the pub we suddenly heard a police siren. We all piled out and saw one police car pulling up outside the jewellers. The two coppers inside the car must have been shocked by the sight of 2,000 football supporters crowding the High Street of this little sleepy village at 8.30 on a Saturday night. Anyway, they were on the blower, and next thing about ten panda cars screeched round the corner. Everybody began making their way back to the train then, because somebody had said the train was nearly fixed. The next main-line station was Crewe and all the scallies knew there would be a reception committee waiting to search everybody on the train. So, once again, the cord got pulled enabling the ones with gear to get off the train before it reached Crewe station. As soon as we got into the station the CID were on the train, sniffing around. In those days, they still wore trilbies, drain-pipe trousers and suede shoes and looked like something out of Z Cars. There was a lad sitting near to us, who had robbed three rings, and he turned to his mate and said, 'They won't fucking get me - I've stashed them up my arse!' Little did he know, there was a plain-clothes CID copper sitting right opposite him, as he said it. He got dragged off the train, straightaway. Everybody was laughing as this fella was being frog-marched down the platform, accompanied by these two CID fellas, dressed in trilbies and long overcoats.

JOHN GRIFFITHS
Unemployed joiner

Pre-season tournament,
Amsterdam, 1977

Being an Evertonian, the only reason I went on this particular trip was through knowing the author, who I was mates with. At the time, most of my mates were Liverpudlians anyway, and so I thought, 'Why not go along - anything for a laugh.' Most of the lads I met up with were good lads, anyway, though at first none of them, apart from Eddie, knew that I was an Evertonian. We booked our tickets on Transalpino, and set off from Lime Street on a Sunday afternoon in early August. To be honest, I never missed an Everton home game but I hadn't been to many away games with the Blues. But, during this trip to Amsterdam, my eyes were opened to the fun which could be had following your team, away from home - especially in Europe!

I got an inkling of this as soon as we walked into Lime Street because there was one lad there who had come on the trip with nothing - no change of clothes, no food, no money - nothing, whatsoever! This lad eventually bunked all the way to Amsterdam and back without paying a penny in fares. He'd even bunked the bus from Cantril Farm to Lime Street, in the first place. I believe he went fucking mad on the way home when the bus driver charged him his fare for the journey back to Cantril Farm, after arriving back in Liverpool. The same fella, by the way, came back with more money than any of us put together, having made a killing, selling jeans, shirts and shoes which he had robbed from various shops and boutiques in Amsterdam.

On the train journey down to London I got talking about football with one of the lads. He was asking if I'd been to Chelsea and West Ham, last season? I didn't want to confess to being an Evertonian, for fear of getting ribbed, so I just said, 'No I missed that game,' before hastily adding by way of explanation, 'Because I was working that day.' All the lads present went to all the away games, so I guess he'd marked me down as a bit of a gobshite. I felt like saying to him, 'I'm a fucking Evertonian, you bastard!' All the lads were having a drink and enjoying little sing-songs. I think that song, Poor Scouser Tommy, had just come out, and they were singing that. We made it across London to Liverpool Street Station without mishap, even though none of us had valid tickets for the London underground. Eventually, we made it onto the boat, which left from Harwich late on Sunday night. On the boat itself, the camaraderie among the lads was terrific. Everybody was in the same boat, I suppose, (excuse the pun), and it was a case of sharing everything you had. If somebody robbed food it would be shared among as many people as possible. If ale got robbed then the bottle would be passed around the group. One incident sticks in the mind, when one of the lads produced a wholesale tin of baked beans, like the type you would get in school. Everybody was starving and so we all tucked into this huge can of beans. It was like a clip from Blazing Saddles with everybody in our group taking turns to fart, as loudly as possible after we'd finished the tin off. I also remember that the shutters had been pulled down on a food cabinet which put the blocks on any food being pinched. You could actually see the food itself, but the gap in between the shutters was only three inches wide. But somebody, who was a lot cleverer than me, managed to grab a piece of food, take a bite out of it, and another bite, and another, until he could fit the remaining piece of food through the metal grille. You had to laugh at the ingenuity of it, but, when you're starving, I suppose you would do anything to eat.

We finally docked in Hook of Holland in the early hours of Monday morning and then we piled onto the train to Amsterdam. Most of us present were carrying the *"Scousers suitcase"*, which consisted of a plastic bag containing a couple of cans of ale, which had been robbed from the and a couple of soggy sandwiches, which your mam had made before you left Liverpool. By this time, we all felt dirty, and so we elected to get a good wash-down in one of the fountains in the city centre. We must have attracted some strange looks from the local Dutch people, as the sight of 30 football supporters washing their dirty socks in public, on a Monday afternoon, couldn't have been a common occurrence. We went for something to eat and I had a bit of trouble trying to explain to this hot-dog fella that I wanted brown sauce on my hot-dog. He kept saying, 'You want mayonnaise, on your filling?' And I was saying, 'No, you stupid bastard, I want brown sauce, on it!' Because of my Scouse accent, he couldn't understand a word I was saying. In the end I just took the hot-dog off him and walked away without paying for it. He didn't chase after me, which I thought he would. Instead, he shouted down the street, 'You English bastards, I fucking kill you, one day!'

The tournament, which was being played over three days, was between Liverpool, AZ 67, Barcelona and Ajax. The tickets for the first day's games had a red border around the edges and somebody found out that the tickets for the play-off and final itself two days later were exactly the same but without the red border. So, all we did for those second set of games was to fold the edges of the ticket, so that no red markings were showing. Most of us had managed to get free tickets for the first game, anyway, after we traipsed into Liverpool's training headquarters, which was right next to the Olympic stadium, itself. Tommy Smith was handing out tickets to all-comers, after the players had finished training. Even though I was an Evertonian, I was still excited about mixing with the Liverpool players, which we all did after they had been showered and changed. I had to laugh at Joey Jones, because he was having a sly cigarette behind the dressing rooms. He even said, 'Do us a favour, lads, keep an eye out for Bob Paisley, will you, he doesn't like me smoking!'

Come the day of the game, we found that there were two sets of gates you had to pass through to enter the stadium. You're ticket was checked by a steward and a policeman at the first gate and then you had to enter through a proper turnstile to get into the ground. All the lads had passed through that first gate but, for some unknown reason, I was having some difficulty trying to convince the steward that my ticket was valid. He must have been thinking, 'That fucker's an Evertonian, don't let him in.' In the end, through sheer desperation, I told him that I'd just paid over the odds for my ticket, off a tout, around the corner. He must have thought, 'This fella's fucking nuts, the ground's half empty, anyway.' In the end, they waved me through the gate and I went inside the stadium, where I met up with the lads. I don't remember much about the matches themselves but I recall the trouble which took place after the second set of games, two days later. The Ajax and AZ supporters all ganged up to confront the 500 or so Scousers that were congregated at one end of the stadium. As we walked out, some big Scouser, shouted, 'Whatever you do, stay together!' The Liverpool mob began descending these stone stairs and, next thing, bottles and bricks started raining down on us. We managed to make it to the bottom of the stairwell, though one or two Scousers got hit by flying glass on the way down. When we reached the open area we saw a mob of about 1,000 Dutch supporters, coming toward us. There was nowhere to run and so we charged at them. Luckily, they ran a few hundred yards before re-grouping and charging at us. Fists and boots piled in as the hard-cases battled at the front of each mob. Next thing, the Liverpool crew started throwing bottles and bricks which they had picked up from the floor. Luckily, this had the effect of scaring the Dutch supporters off for a precious few minutes. Time enough for the majority of our mob to run for the trams which were waiting at the top of the street. We all got on, though we were quickly pursued by their mob, who proceeded to brick the windows in the trams. There was glass flying everywhere and one or two of their mob actually tried to climb on. We managed to kick them off before screaming at the driver to get going. He was all for going on strike, there and then, but luckily, had the presence of mind to drive us out of there. I'm telling you, it was a scary situation to be in.

That night, we slept on one of those glass-topped cruise boats that were moored at the side of the canal. There were about 20 of us lying on the floor of this boat. It must have been around 2am when we'd all settled down for the night. For some reason, I couldn't sleep and so I was lying there, not knowing what to expect next, and I was looking up at the sky through the glass roof when, suddenly, the buildings on the quayside started moving. I thought, 'Some bastard's took the fucking rope off.' I jumped up in panic, shouting, 'Quick, get off, we're fucking moving!' I was half-way through the door when I realised the rope had three foot of slack which allowed it to move backwards and forwards with the tide. With all the shouting and panicking, I'd woken everybody up. 'You stupid bastard,' they were calling me. It's a good job they didn't know I was an Evertonian otherwise they probably would have thrown me fucking overboard. But, we finally got our heads down for the night and everybody slept surprisingly well, considering the discomfort of our surroundings.

The next day, we went looking for presents to take home. Thing was, nobody had any money so we went on a shoplifting expedition. I robbed a lovely silver plated clog which had a lighter on the front of it. I was made up with it and said to myself, 'I'll give that to my dad, he'll be made up with that.' But, on the train on the way home some bastard went rooting through my bag and swapped this lighter for a shitty wooden one, which fell apart as soon as you tried to light it. I was going fucking mad but, I suppose, it could have been worse. He could have taken the lighter and left me with nothing. Or, taken the lighter and left me with a box of fucking matches.

On the boat home we actually got talking to Bobby Robson, and two of his players, Brian Talbot and Alan Brazil. They were part of the Ipswich Town squad who were coming home from a pre-season tournament in Belgium. The three of them were having a drink in the bar and I got talking to them. After a while, Bobby Robson left, but the two ers stayed to have a bevvy with us. We were talking football and I asked Bryan Talbot about Brian Hamilton, who was playing for Everton, at the time. He was a former team-mate of his at Ipswich Town and he told us that Hamilton's legs were on the way out, and that's why the East Anglian club had let him go.

We got off the boat at Harwich and then travelled home via Liverpool Street Station and London underground, before catching the train to Lime Street, and home. Even though I was an Evertonian, the whole trip, from start to finish, was brilliant and I made some good friends with the Liverpudlians I met.

● ● ● ● ● ● ● ● ● ● ● ● ● ● ● ● ●

TONY HOBSON
Unemployed Labourer

Wolverhampton Wanderers v Liverpool,
League title decider, May, 1976

I was still at school when this game was played in 1976. I was in class 5T of St. Teresa's in Norris Green. Myself and four of my mates, who were all in the same class, decided to bunk off school in order to go to the match. To be honest, there was no way we would have missed it for the world, anyway. All the talk for days before was this Wolves game and how we were going to bunk off school without attracting the wrath of our teachers and parents. None of us cared about any punishment which might come our way because the game was too important to miss. On the morning of the match we all went to school as normal, but didn't bother going in through the schoolgates. What we did was to go back home and all we said was, 'Mam, I've been sent home!' The funny thing was, nobody's Mam or Dad questioned us at all. They probably knew we had

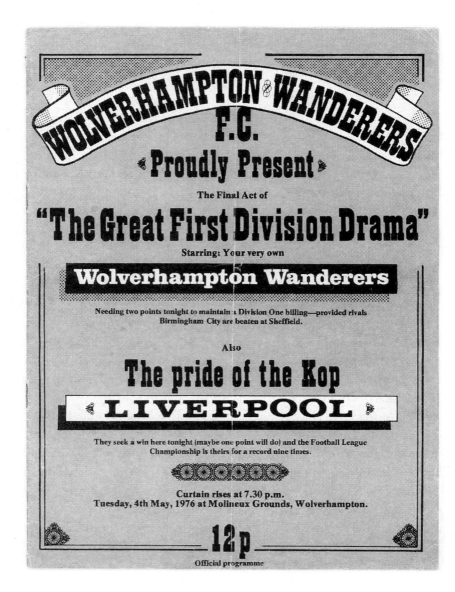

our hearts set on going to the game. So, we met up at the Western pub about 10am, in good time to walk to the East Lancs Road, where we planned to hitch a lift to Wolverhampton. We were standing on the corner, by Lower Lane police station, for about ten minutes when a bottle green mini-van pulled up. It turned out it was a fella and his son, who lived just three streets away from where we lived. They were going to the game themselves and they took us all the way to the centre of Wolverhampton. On the way down the motorway we stopped at one of the service stations. None of us had much money, though. I think, between the five of us, we had £2 in our pockets. But funnily enough, we managed to get lots of freebies that day, which kept the hunger pains away at least. We arrived in Wolverhampton at around midday and because none of us had any money for a ticket we made straight for the ground to suss out our little bunking-in route for when the gates opened later that day. Arriving at the ground we couldn't believe the scene which greeted us. There were literally thousands of Liverpool supporters already queuing up. All around the ground and in the surrounding streets it was just a mass of red and white. There wasn't one policeman in sight, either, but everything was orderly - there was no trouble whatsoever. Then somebody shouted, 'Come on, let's get into the ground, now!' The gates got kicked in and hundreds ran onto the terraces. We thought, 'This is great, we've got our spec, we'll stay here until the match starts.' Next thing, about 200 policemen came running toward us from Molineux's home end. It ended up like something out of the Keystone Kops, with the policemen chasing hundreds of Liverpool supporters all around the ground. In the end, even they saw the funny side of the situation. My mates and I ended up walking into the city centre where we got rigged out in new trainers, T-shirts, jeans and Wrangler jackets. We managed to sell a couple of pairs of jeans and T-shirts to Liverpool supporters which helped cover our expenses for the day. After having our tea in a cafe in the town centre we made our way to the ground about 5.30pm. On the journey all you could see were thousands of Liverpool supporters walking toward Molineux. What sticks in my mind, though, was seeing

Gayle, who was playing for Liverpool at the time, on crutches, struggling to get to the ground in time for the start of the match. Having arrived we wondered how we were going to get in to see the game. This problem was solved when one of the gates suddenly burst open, letting in hundreds of Liverpool supporters for free. My mates and I soon joined the throng and pretty soon we were standing on the big away terrace with all the other Liverpudlians. Saying that, there were Reds supporters all around Molineux that night. The paddock was full of Liverpool; both stands seemed full of them, too. The home end was the only place where the Wolves supporters were able to congregate, but about 30 minutes before

kick-off another load of Liverpool supporters suddenly started appearing on their terrace. There were a couple of scuffles between the two sets of fans but, in the end, sanity prevailed and the protagonists were content to stand off from each other. With the minutes ticking away before kick-off the atmosphere inside the ground was beginning to get electric. The Liverpool supporters were really making themselves heard around Molineux. Ten minutes before the teams came out onto the pitch a Wolves supporter ran from their end toward the centre circle. He stopped and suddenly beckoned the Liverpool fans to come and fight him. The challenge was taken up by a called Jimmy, from Norris Green. Punches were traded in the centre circle before another Wolves supporter ran on to join in the fight. Another lad from Norris Green, called Lolla, then ran on and began fighting with him. The crowd were booing and cheering as each punch was thrown. To the delight of the away fans, Liverpool won the boxing contest 2-0 and the conquering hero's made a safe journey back to the terraces before the police could grab hold of them.

The two teams finally came out to a crescendo of noise which raised the roof off the ground. The match itself was one of the best I've ever seen with Wolves taking the lead, through Steve Kindon, in the first half. The second half was a different story with the Reds scoring three times without reply to secure the League title. The scenes afterwards were unbelievable with thousands of Liverpudlians running onto the pitch to celebrate. It was party-time, both inside and outside the ground, after that. Everybody was cheering and singing, 'We've won the League, ee aye adio, we've won the League.' My mates and I ended up walking down this road, where we managed to hitch a lift to the M6 motorway. The traffic on the motorway itself stretched for miles. There were thousands of Liverpudlians standing on the hard shoulder, singing, dancing and passing bottles of whisky around. Everybody was having a ball. People travelling on the south-bound carriageway were actually getting out of their cars to watch the scene as the Liverpool fans continued singing and dancing all over the M6 motorway. We walked along the hard shoulder, knocking on every window, asking for a lift. Eventually, a Liverpool supporter said, 'Get in here, lads,' and we climbed in. We arrived home about 3.30am and went straight to bed, tired but happy. The next morning, me Mam shouted at me for getting in late. I expected worse when I arrived at school, though. All five of us walked into the classroom at the same time, expecting our teacher to go berserk. But all she said was, 'Take a seat, lads, and try and catch up on the work you missed, yesterday.' We were made up because we hadn't expected such a walkover. Thing is, I would happily have taken six of the best just to be at Molineux for that

TONY HOBSON
Unemployed Labourer

Glasgow Celtic v Liverpool,
Benefit game for Hillsborough families,
Celtic Park, April 1989

A friend of ours, Harold Hughes, who would 'mind' the Liverpool players whenever they got into a bit of bother with club doormen, or whatever, had arranged for a gang of us to travel from the Bridge Inn, in Broadway, early on Sunday morning. We arrived in Glasgow around dinner-time and soon bumped into Harold's son, who informed us of a 'celebrity party' which was taking place in the Gorbals after the game. The Gorbals was supposed to be a dodgy area of Glasgow but we agreed to go. 'And before you go there,' he said, 'get yourselves down to the Albany Hotel, because the Liverpool and Celtic players will be having a drink in there after the game.' So, our day was sorted out. We'd go to the match, then onto the Albany Hotel, before leaving for the party in the Gorbals.

Arriving at Celtic Park we were struck by the friendliness of the Celtic supporters. They couldn't have been more welcoming with the few thousand Liverpool supporters who had made the trip to Glasgow. We were in a queue for the refreshment bar and Celtic supporters, who were at the front of the queue, on seeing us dressed in red and white waved us to the front. They were coming over to us with cans of ale, shaking our hands and saying hello. Even in the Jungle, the notorious home end at Celtic Park, the welcome couldn't have been better. Celtic supporters were lifting young Liverpool fans onto their shoulders so the kids could see the game properly. We were situated in the stand opposite the Jungle and we could see small pockets of red and white in different parts of the Jungle terracing and there wasn't any trouble. As I say, the Celtic supporters really went out of their way to make every Liverpool fan feel at home that day. When the Celtic crowd sang, You'll Never Walk Alone, the singing must have been heard about five miles away. I've never known the Kop at Anfield sing it any better than the Celtic supporters did that day.

After the game it was a mad dash back to the Albany Hotel because we'd been told by Harold's son that if we got there handy, before the players arrived, we would be in - no bother. But, we couldn't find the hotel, at first, but eventually, we did. As we were pulling up in a taxi, Bob Paisley and a couple of the Liverpool directors were going into the hotel entrance. Now, our favourite trick to get into a party such as this was to have a pen which didn't write. Anyway, we walked up to Bob Paisley and asked, 'Any chance of your autograph, please Bob?' before walking through the door of the hotel with him. He knew what was going on but all he did was to smile and say, 'Go and take a seat lads, be quiet, and you'll be okay.' So, we were sitting in the foyer having a drink, just biding our time before trying to bunk our way past the Beefeater, who, by this stage, was busy reading out the name's of the players as they made their way, one by one, into the main room. We were thinking, 'How are we going to get in there, past this fella?' One of my mates then had the bright idea of walking up to him and saying, 'I'm Paul Aldridge, John's brother.' He got nodded in. So we went through all the Scousers in the team, pretending to be relations of them. I was Steve McMahon's brother. Another lad was Gary Ablett's cousin. And that's how we got into the party. But, as soon as we walked into the room we knew we were going to get sussed, straightaway, because there were exactly 45 seats, enough to seat the Liverpool and Celtic players, staff and directors, but not us. We were standing at the bar and it was looking odds-on that we were going to get lashed out. Bob Paisley must have seen what was going on and he came over and said, 'Listen lads, you can't stay here, it's going to get a bit sticky for you. Why don't you have a drink in the other bar and I'll send the players in, after the meal.' We took Bob's advice and went next door where we had a drink with the player's wives. We were talking with Marina Dalglish and she was really friendly with us. Gary Ablett's wife

over and we were talking to her for ages. Talking with the player's wives backed up our original story in the eyes of the Beefeater, who was watching us like a hawk. Next thing, Marti Pellow from Wet, Wet, Wet, walked in. He'd been booked to sing to the player's wives while the players themselves had their meal, in the other room. But before he began singing, he had a bevvy with us and he was a sound guy - really down to earth. Harold Hughes, himself, walked in then, shouting, 'What's going on here then, where's the lads?' A couple of the players replied, 'They're in the other room, Harold.' He said, 'No, I mean the lads!' And he came barging over, got us a bevvy and sat down. Before we knew it, all the Liverpool team were sitting around our table chatting to us. We were all having a good time, drinking and talking about football when suddenly Craig Johnston walked in. As soon as he did, the atmosphere went dead. We're thinking, 'Hang on, he's a red, what's going on here?' It was later on we found out that the players wouldn't talk to him because of what he'd said on the eve of the cup final against Wimbledon the previous year. If you remember, he'd announced his intention to retire from football the day before the game, which had caused the club a certain amount of embarrassment, at the time. This was the first time he'd met up with the Liverpool squad since that day. Craig ended up sitting with us, having a drink. Marti Pellow came back and sat with us then. He wouldn't let us buy a drink, at all. We had a good couple of hours with Marti and then it was time to make our way to the party in the Gorbals. But before that Craig Johnston treated us to a meal, in a nice restaurant, around the corner from the hotel. All of us, including Craig, then left for the party. When we arrived at the pub, I noticed that there were shutters and big bolts enclosing all the windows. I'm thinking, 'What are we doing here, we're gonna get fleeced.' Harold, being who he was, had gone into the pub, and, I presumed, had said something to the people in there because these two big doormen came out and told us straight, 'You can leave your keys in the ignition, leave all your windows open, throw £50 on the seat and there will not be anything touched by the time you come out.' Craig Johnston had a minder with him, a fella called Bridgey, who lived in

Sandfield Park, in West Derby. He was driving a Mercedes and neither his or anybody else's car got scratched. The party itself was being thrown for Harold and his Glasgow mates. The local people were really nice to us to a point where two old ladies left the party only to come back ten minutes later with roast dinners which they had cooked for us earlier. The party finally broke up after much singing and dancing in the early hours of Monday morning. It ended up with five of us travelling back to Liverpool in the Mercedes with Craig Johnston rotten drunk in the back seat.

● ● ● ● ● ● ● ● ● ● ● ● ● ● ● ● ●

JOHN WEBSTER
Office Clerk

Sheffield Wednesday v Liverpool
League game, Hillsborough, November, 1965

My very first away game was at Sheffield Wednesday in the 1965/66 season. Liverpool won the game 2-0 with Roger Hunt and Peter Thompson scoring the goals. I was still a pupil at the Collegiate School, in Shaw Street, at the time, and a group of schoolmates and I booked our tickets on Crown coaches, which cost us about 7/6d. The most vivid recollection of the day was actually passing the sight of the Moors Murders, on the journey to Sheffield. You could see the uniformed bobbies, armed with spades, searching the moors, as we drove by. On the outskirts of Sheffield the older fellas on the coach started having a laugh and this involved opening the windows of the coach, which you could do in those days, and grabbing bottles of milk from a stationary float, which was held up at traffic lights. Once they had polished off the milk the fans just threw the empty bottles out of the windows. Nothing changes, does it! At the time it was all very exciting, of course. I was only 11 years of age and all these shenanigans were new to me. And, of course, I wanted to be a part of it. So, I threw a bottle out of the window as well, just to hard in front of my mates, ha, ha!

The bus eventually got stopped by the police and all the fans were questioned for about half an hour before they finally let us go, without arresting anybody. We arrived at the ground to the sound of 'Liverpool, Liverpool!' as hundreds of Liverpudlians were milling around Hillsborough. My mates and I had a look around the ground, bought fish and chips and a programme and went into the away end of the ground, the Leppings Lane end. We thought that was where most of the Liverpool supporters would be congregated but we were in for a shock because, looking across the pitch, all we saw was red and white favours in a big arc, all around the terracing behind the opposite goal. They must have filled at least half of the big open end at Hillsborough. You could see the Sheffield Wednesday supporters, having been pushed away from the area behind the goal, all congregating on the outside terracing, near the sides and back. There was no trouble at all. It's just that there were so many Liverpudlians in that end of the ground that they automatically dominated the terraces. When the teams came out, to a great cheer, all you could see were thousands of raised hands clapping and Scouse voices singing, 'Oh, when the Saints, go marching in, oh when the Saints go marching in, I wanna be in that number, oh, when the Saints go marching in.' Ian St. John was in the team, of course, and that's why the Liverpool supporters used to sing, 'Saints,' instead of 'Reds,' to that particular song.

I know it sounds corny now but, as a kid, it was great to be a member of Shankly's Red Army, which is what we were known as. Thousands of Liverpool fans would travel to every away game to see the team play. They always made plenty of noise as well, often out-shouting the home supporters. Not many other clubs' fans had their own songs, in those days, but the Liverpool fans had their own song-book, which they sang at each away game. Before this Sheffield Wednesday game, I'd only ever been to Anfield with my parents and so, to be away from home for the first t   i   m   e   , was certainly an eye-opener. The antics of the fans on the coach was really exciting for an 11 year old. There was even a gang-bang on the way home when this girl, who must have been about 17, started necking with this fella. We were sneaking a look when suddenly the couple started really getting into it, on the back seat of the coach. She was lying there as he did the business, not really caring who was looking. When he'd finished she still lay there, with her legs wide open, inviting all the lads to have a go. In the end, she did a turn for six fellas, while my mates and I watched eagerly from the sidelines. While we were busy ogling her this spotty faced fella turned to me and said, 'Go on mate, give her one!' I looked at him and I looked at the girl, or rather her fanny, which by this stage was looking a bit like the Mersey Tunnel it was so wide, and I said, 'No, I don't want to.' Truth is, my little widgy would probably have gotten lost in there, after all the shafting her fanny had already taken. I got home that night and the first thing my parents asked was, 'How did you're day go, son?' I couldn't tell them half the things which had gone on so I just said, 'Oh, great, Liverpool were brilliant and we deserved to win!'

• • • • • • • • • • • • • • • • •

JOHN WEBSTER
Office Clerk

Manchester United v Liverpool,
League game, Old Trafford, April, 1972

In those halcyon days of the sixties and, to an extent, the seventies, you could look up to the players. These days, I wouldn't give half of them the time of day. You look at the money the Liverpool players are earning today and you watch them playing and you can see they're not trying half the time. You can slag them off for that but, at the end of the day, it's the club itself which you love, not the players who are representing it. Liverpool Football Club is what you believe in as an institution, not individual players. In this respect, Bill Shankly was a very special person because he managed to breed a tremendous sense of value and discipline among the players and I think this aspect of man-management is missing these days - at all clubs, not just Liverpool. I hear certain things which the players get up to in clubs and to me this is wrong. If a sportsman like Linford Christie had a 100 metre race to run on Saturday then I'm sure he wouldn't go gallivanting around clubs on the piss a couple of days before the event. To me, this is the difference between players of today and their counterparts from an earlier age. And, for that reason, I could never admire some of today's top footballers, because, to me, they're not worth a carrot.

Even the support they get from the fans themselves is different these days. I know this is going to sound a bit bolshie, but I look upon myself as a real Liverpool fan, simply because I was supporting them before they had won all those European Cups, FA Cups and League Championships. Because of our success I believe there are a lot of hangers-on following Liverpool, these days. If, for example, Tranmere Rovers had won all those cups then I'm certain those same out-of-town fans, who currently support us, would be supporting the Birkenhead club, simply because they would be classed as a glamorous and successful side. If Liverpool were in the Third Division now, then there is no way you would see coach after coach coming up the M62 to see them play. I know people are entitled to support any team they want but I sometimes wonder where these out-of-town supporters were, or where their father's and mother's were, when Liverpool were in the Second Division, throughout most of the 1950's. Certainly not at Anfield, that's for sure! And, to me, that's the underlying difference between home-based support and out-of-town support. You see whole families turning up to watch Liverpool at Anfield, dressed from head to foot in the team kit, and, to be honest, I wonder where they get the money from to rig themselves out like that. Football becoming a family-orientated game, which, in many ways, is a great shame because it has diluted the passion of the fans to such an extent that, at times, you can hear a pin drop at Anfield. For somebody brought up on the Kop in the 1960's that is a phenomena which truly saddens me.

I mentioned football's by-gone age just now and life as a football supporter was so much better in those days. It was cheaper to get into the ground, cheaper to travel to away games. In that last respect British Rail used to run special trains from Lime Street to every town and city in the country. Those trains would be packed to the rafters with Liverpool fans supporting their team, no matter what ground they were travelling to; be it St. James Park, Upton Park, Stamford Bridge or Roker Park. There was very little segregation and scarcely any trouble, at any ground. I say scarcely because the only place I ever encountered such tension was at Old Trafford. There always seemed to be an intimidating atmosphere at that place. I don't know why. Maybe it was because of the close proximity of the two cities. But, then again, I never encountered any trouble at Maine Road, so maybe it was just plain jealousy on the part of the Manchester United supporters. As I say, there was always a real ugly atmosphere inside Old Trafford whenever they played Liverpool. In those days, Liverpool's away support was predominantly male-based. Consequently, if there was any trouble then it tended to get sorted out, quickly. You very rarely encountered home fans waiting at train stations for you - there were usually too many Liverpool supporters for them to contend with. But the exception was always Old Trafford. For this particular game, which the Red-men won 3-0, with goals from Chris Lawler, John Toshack and Emlyn Hughes, the trouble began even before we'd reached Victoria Station, on the special train which had left Lime Street at 12 noon. A huge cob of metal, the size of a football crashed into the window of one of the carriages just outside Patricroft, a suburb of Manchester. It hit a Liverpool supporter right on the head, and, I swear, I thought he was dead. There was blood pouring everywhere; on the seats, on his clothes, on the floor of the carriage. I felt sorry for the poor fella but he got looked after when the train arrived in Victoria Station. There must have been about 600 Liverpool supporters, mostly young fellas, marching out of the station concourse, ready for the three mile walk to Old Trafford. We knew there would be Manchester United fans waiting for us, but we were ready to fight anybody. Next thing, a mob of about 70 of their supporters ran out of this alehouse across the road and started throwing bricks and bottles at us. The Liverpool mob charged them down the street only to be confronted by the biggest mob I've ever seen in my life. There must have been about 800 of them, all armed with bricks, hammers, bottles, you name it, they had your name on it. The Liverpool mob started walking back toward Victoria Station, in order to escape from their mob. We made it back, just! Only to be chased back into the street by the police with dogs. By now, there was nothing to be done but to run the gauntlet all the way up to the ground. It was every man for himself as fellas took hidings, left, right and centre. Don't get me wrong, the Liverpool mob had a go at them, but being in a strange town and with so many of them to contend with, we were fighting a losing battle. Out of the 600 who set out from Victoria Station, less than 50 survived the three mile journey to Old Trafford. I ended up going into the Stretford End because I surmised it would be much safer in there than it would have been in the Scoreboard End. That was where the main Liverpool support was congregated and also where the Manchester United hooligan element gathered. Because of that, you just knew there would be aggro on the terraces. I was standing next to old fellas in the Stretford End and, as the fists and boots were flying in the Scoreboard End you could hear them shouting, 'Get into the Scouse bastards!' I was shocked by the level of hatred directed at us and, for that reason, I've never been that keen to go to Old Trafford since. Liverpool played really well in this game but there was no appreciation of our performance from their supporters. When teams played well at Anfield the crowd wouldn't hesitate to applaud their efforts. But the Manchester United supporters, young and old alike, would never give you any credit. In all my time watching football I've never met such an unsporting and unappreciative crowd.

After the game I managed to catch a train right outside the ground which took me straight to the centre of town. I was one of the first Liverpool supporters back and I witnessed the Liverpool fans coming back in one's and two's, all black and blue, from whacks they had received from the home supporters. That put me off going to the game for a while but, apparently, the Manchester United supporters got their comeuppance when they came to Anfield the following season, when hundreds of our fans chased the Manchester United crowd all the way down Scotland Road.

● ● ● ● ● ● ● ● ● ● ● ● ● ● ● ●

JOHN SWIFT
Plessey's

AS Roma v Liverpool
European Cup Final, Rome,
May 1984

These days I'm a steward on match-days at Anfield, which I started doing in January 1996. What happened was, I filled in the form, which one of my mates, who was already a steward, gave me. I filled it in not expecting to hear anything because, apparently, there's a big queue for steward's jobs at Anfield. At the same time, I was playing football for Plessey's in the Zingari Alliance League on Saturday's which would have curtailed my appearances at Anfield, anyway. But with Liverpool playing most of their games on Sunday or Monday night's for the rest of the season, I was able to take the job. The ironic thing was, my cartilage went playing football just after Christmas and I had to retire from playing, anyway, because of the injury to my knee. A week after filling in the form I got a telephone call asking me to report for duty for the Nottingham

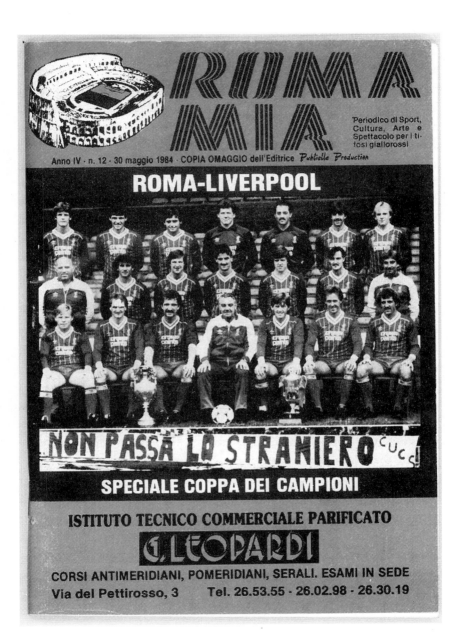

Forest game in January. It's a great job for a Liverpudlian because you're able to watch the game for nothing and get paid a tenner for your troubles. Obviously, there is work to do but you find that, on the whole, the crowds at Anfield are very well behaved. Now and again you might get away supporters running onto the pitch from the Anfield Road end when their team has scored, but, by and large, there is very little trouble. My main job is to ensure that supporters don't come into the ground carrying any alcohol or offensive weapons. I must say, it's very rare you will have a problem, in this respect. As I say, it's the best job around, because after ten past three, when everybody is more or less seated, we can settle down to watch the match. One game which sticks in my mind, since I've become a steward, is the Newcastle game last season, which Liverpool won. When the score was 3-2 to Newcastle, I remember walking past the bench, where the managers sit, and Kevin Keegan was up and down, at every incident on the pitch. I shouted to him, 'Watch your blood pressure there, Kevin!' He shook his head, winced, and shouted back, 'Oh, I know, yes!' When Stan Collymore struck the winner I was standing ten feet away from the Kop, in front of the paddock, and I automatically turned toward the crowd as the ball flew into the net. I had my arms spread wide, in a stopping motion to any would-be on the pitch merchants, but really I was celebrating the fact that we'd scored. In the excitement, all these fellas started jumping on me. The head steward ran over from the Kop, thinking I was getting attacked. I just said to him, 'Don't worry, I was only helping these lads to celebrate.'

It is moments like that, as well as the trip I'm about to describe, which sum up, to me, what being a Liverpool supporter is all about. My brother Brian and I booked two coach tickets on Home James, a local company, for this trip to Rome for the European Cup Final. The tickets themselves cost us £80, which didn't include a hotel, or anything like that. It was the basic coach journey to Italy and back. The prospect of such a long journey didn't bother me in the slightest because, unfortunately, I'd had to miss the first European Cup Final in 1977 because I'd just got married a couple of weeks before and couldn't afford the fare to Rome, on that occasion. For that reason, I was so looking forward to this game with the prospect of seeing Liverpool lift the European Cup for a fourth time. The journey to Italy was pretty uneventful, which was surprising considering the reputation for thieving which Scousers were renowned for. The only incident of any note came on the Switzerland/Italian border after we'd stopped at a service station for refreshments. There was a big shopping mall situated alongside and the Liverpool supporters made a bee-line for this, of course. But beforehand, we had all been warned by our coach-driver that if there was any nonsense he would turn back, straightaway. So, after we'd all bought something to eat at the service station we got back onto the coach and settled back for the final leg of our journey. Suddenly, our driver found himself being waved down by two Italian policemen, telling him to stop the coach. Next thing, all these Italian coppers were searching our coach, looking for stolen gear. As far as we knew, nobody had robbed anything at all from the service station. It was then we found out that a tracksuit had gone missing from one of the sports shops in the shopping mall. To be honest, for a coach-load of Liverpool supporters, I thought that was pretty reasonable. But our coach-driver took a different view, saying, 'That's it, I'm turning the bus round and taking the fucking lot of you home, now!' We were all panicking, of course, thinking that we wouldn't see the game. Luckily, it turned out that there was a practising solicitor on board our coach and he got off to talk to the police. Five minutes later he came back and told us that the Italian police were willing to forget the whole incident if the tracksuit turned up. They let everybody off the coach while they searched for the stolen tracksuit. When they found it they just smiled, told us to get back on board and then waved us onto the motorway, and that was the end of that saga.

We eventually arrived in Rome around 11pm on Tuesday, the night before the game. With having no accommodation we were wondering where to get our heads down. By this time, our kid and I had latched onto some of the other Liverpool supporters from our coach and so about ten of us decided to find a bar in the centre of Rome. We left our belongings on the coach and the driver said, 'I'll pick you up outside the ground, after the match, tomorrow night.' We said, 'Fine, we'll see you then,' and went for a bevvy. We went wandering around Rome until we eventually found this bar, which sold the world's most expensive lager. They must have seen us coming because they charged us £25pounds for five pints of lager. We drank up and paid for the drinks and then went looking for a bar where the ale was cheaper. We ended up in this bar next to the Ritz hotel. There were loads of Liverpool supporters in there and so we settled down to have a good time. Around 1.30am people were starting to think of places where they could get their heads down for the night. There was a door on the other side of the bar which led to the hotel foyer and one by one the Liverpudlians were making their way through there. We wondered where they were going so we finished our lager and followed them through this door. It turned out the guy who was in charge of the hotel was letting Liverpool supporters sleep on the couches and carpets in the hotel foyer. When we got in there the place was already full of Scouser's lying on chairs and couches. The floor was literally covered with sleeping football fans. You couldn't move and so our kid, this other fella and myself, sneaked into the lift up to the third floor and got our heads down in the corridor. Unknown to us, the hotel manager had opened a reception room at the back of the hotel, to allow even more Liverpool fans to come into his hotel, for free. Us three were sleeping in a corridor on the third floor when we could have had a three seater couch each if only we had stayed downstairs for a bit longer. But we were grateful for the chance to sleep in some comfort because a lot of Liverpool supporters were walking the streets all night.

The next morning, when we came downstairs, there were Liverpool supporters all over the hotel foyer. There were a load of Americans in the restaurant, by this time, and they complained to the management that they couldn't eat their breakfast in peace. The relief manager acted upon their wishes and threw us all out onto the street. This was about 7am and so we went for something to eat and then had a walk around the city. By chance, the three of us ventured upon a football game which was about to take place between the British press and Italian press in a stadium which was about the size of Tranmere Rover's ground. There was about two hours to go before kick off and everybody was milling around by the main entrance to the stadium. This Irish journalist suddenly came up to us and asked, 'Do any of you lads fancy a game, our team are short?' We said, 'We haven't brought any boots or kit.' He said, 'Don't worry, we can provide those for you.' Our kid and I were made up at the chance of playing alongside some of the big names in football journalism. Unfortunately, a car suddenly pulled up and five British journalists jumped out, explaining, 'Sorry we're late, got held up in the traffic.' So, that was that, the team was suddenly oversubscribed and we had to forsake our celebrity game of football.

The rest of the day was spent sightseeing - I think we covered Rome in about two hours. By this time other lads had latched onto us so there were about 15 of us, in all. We nicknamed ourselves, B Company. We ended up by the Trevi fountain, where Paul Usher, who played Barry Grant in Brookside, was leading the singing on top of the steps. In the end, the authorities turned the fountain off because so many fans were jumping in. We never saw many Roma fans in the daytime, though we saw lots of Lazio supporters. They were really friendly toward us, wishing us all the best and telling us they hoped Liverpool beat their closest rivals.

Around 5pm we jumped a bus to the ground and had a walk round the stadium. There was no trouble at all. The Liverpool supporters were mixing quite freely with the Roma supporters, swapping scarves and banners, and suchlike. There were lots of souvenirs being sold outside the ground including these air-horns, which this Italian trader had piled up on a paste table. The Liverpool fans were buying these air-horns - I think they were about £5. But, as soon as they reached the turnstiles with these things, the police were taking the air-horns off them. Then, every now and again, the policemen would scoop a load of these air-horns into their arms and then carry them over to the trader who would sell them on again to other Liverpool supporters. We were watching what was going on and couldn't believe their cheek. In the end, we started warning the Liverpool supporters not to buy these air-horns because they were wasting their money.

As for the game itself, well, all I remember are those penalties, which were a nightmare to start with. When Steve Nicol blasted the ball over that cross-bar I remember thinking to myself, 'I've come all this fucking way just to see us get beat on penalties.' But, with Roma missing all theirs it was finally down to Alan Kennedy to try and win the European Cup for us with the final penalty. I was debating whether or not to look away but I just had to watch. And when the ball went into the net the feeling was surreal. None of us stopped jumping up and down for about 20 minutes - the feeling was so good. What also gave us great pleasure was beating AS Roma in their own back-yard because all day we'd noticed all kinds of bunting all over the city saying, 'Roma, European Champions, 1984.' This was in preparation for the wild celebrations which were supposed to take place after they had beaten us. But, Liverpool spoilt the party, I'm glad to say. When Graeme Souness lifted the cup you could sense the atmosphere had changed from one of fierce but friendly passion into something war-like. Little fires were being lit on the terraces where the Roma fans were congregated. The Liverpudlians got kept inside the ground for about half an hour after the game. We didn't mind this because we knew there would be mobs waiting for us outside the ground. Eventually, we got filtered out of the ground through this little entrance. On the way out the Italian police were hitting some of the Liverpool supporters with batons, even though the fans concerned hadn't done anything to warrant such a hiding. The Liverpool fans were ushered toward the coach-park where there must have been about 2,000 of us, all waiting to board our coaches. The Roma mobs were there too, trying to single out lone Scousers. Luckily, the police and paratroopers were out in force that night and they managed to protect us from the worst excesses of the Roma supporters. After an hour the majority of coaches from Liverpool began leaving the coach-park with their occupants safely on board. Another hour went by and we still hadn't boarded the coach for the simple reason that ours hadn't turned up. 50 of us were stranded in this coach-park with baying Italian mobs surrounding the perimeters. By this time it was 12 midnight and we were really beginning to panic. Our kid and I walked up to this policeman and explained that our coach hadn't turned up and, frankly, we were shit-scared of being left here, at the mercy of these marauding Italian fans. Good enough, the police were brilliant because as soon as they realised our predicament they went out of their way to help us. They were on their radio's straightaway, trying to locate our coach. No luck in that respect, though, because there was still no sign of it. A couple of them even drove around the city centre trying to find it. Still no luck. In the end they said, 'You two, come with us and you tell us where you're coach dropped you off last night.' Our kid and I jumped into the back of this Fiat police car with my big Liverpool flag which I had to drape out of the window because it was so big. We drove through the centre of Rome and all you could see were cars getting overturned and windows getting smashed by mobs of Roma supporters. I don't know what they thought as we passed by with my huge LFC flag fluttering out of the police car window, but I bet it wasn't very complimentary. We couldn't find the coach so we turned and headed back to the coach-park, which was deserted except for 50, by now, rather tired looking Liverpool supporters. The Italian police eventually laid on a bus to take us to the British Embassy. This was a total waste of time because they didn't want to know us. They wouldn't even let us near the gates of the building. One of them said, in this rather haughty voice, 'Get off those gates, or I'll let the dogs onto you!' Eventually, after much insistence from a senior Italian policeman, they deigned to help us in the morning. We asked the British Embassy official who was standing at the other side of the gate, 'What are we supposed to do, in the meantime.' He said, 'You can stay outside this building but you definitely cannot come inside.' So,

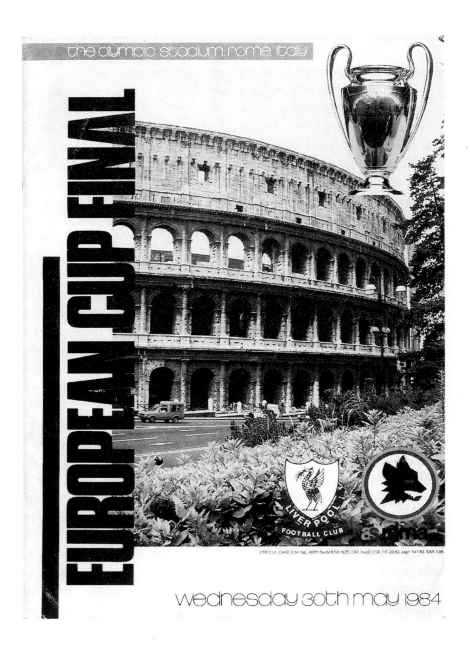

there we all were, 50 of us trying to find a comfortable spec on the pavement outside the British Embassy. We were starving by now and so a gang of us walked to the railway station, which was a few hundred yards up the road, to get something to eat and drink. We saw a few benches on the station concourse and we decided to sleep on these for the night. The next morning the wheels were finally set in motion as they announced that they would get us all home by different methods of transport. Some went home by plane, others travelled back by train and the rest of us by coach. The British Embassy official in charge, announced that there were six seats available on a coach which was due to leave Rome in an hour's time. So, we jumped into a taxi and the driver, knowing we were in a hurry, drove like a lunatic through the streets of Rome. In order to avoid the worst traffic snarl-ups he was driving through parks and narrow alleyways in a frenzied effort to get us to the coach on time. Thanks to him we made it with a couple of minutes to spare.

We made it back to Liverpool around Friday lunch-time and the first port of call was to the offices of Home James, in Picton Road. Luckily, the boss wasn't there. I say luckily because there were fellas with us who were ready to kill him after the messing they had gone through over the past couple of days. The girls in the office were saying, 'We know nothing about this, mate, it's not our fault.' Eventually, we found out what had happened to our coach. It turned out that the coach driver had hightailed it out of Rome as soon as he'd dropped us off on Tuesday night, because, unknown to us, he was booked to take a coach-load of people from Den Haag, in Holland, to England the very next day. For obvious reasons, we weren't told about this unscheduled trip to the northern reaches of Europe. When the boss himself arrived back in the office all he had to say was, 'You all got home, didn't you, what are you worrying about?' The solicitor who had been on our coach said to him, 'I'm taking you to court, on behalf of all these people.' We all threw in £15 to cover the barrister's costs and when the case eventually came to court the driver's version of events was that we trashed the coach to such an extent that he had no alternative but to leave us in Rome while he went and got the coach repaired. Our barrister shot the coach driver down, good style, and then proceeded to put our case forward brilliantly. After a day's deliberation the judge came down in our favour with the result that everyone of us got £250 each as compensation.

● ● ● ● ● ● ● ● ● ● ● ● ● ● ● ● ● ●

JOHN SWIFT
Plessey's

Sunderland v Liverpool,
Roker Park, November, 1976

In an effort to impress my future wife, I decided to take her to watch Liverpool play at Sunderland in the depths of winter. As you know, weather-wise the north east is not the most hospitable of places and you could tell that Joy wasn't impressed with my efforts to please her. We sat in the two seats next to the back seat of the coach. There were a gang of lads sitting at the back of us, all singing and chanting, throughout the journey. There were also a couple of my mates, who had been on the ale the night before, who were still half-drunk when they boarded the coach at 9 o'clock that morning. An hour into the journey and my two mates were both bursting for a pee. Unfortunately, there were no toilets on the coach and the driver, when asked to stop, refused to do so, saying, 'I'm sorry lads, I'm not allowed to stop on the hard shoulder.' By this time, the two lads were desperate to relieve themselves, but there was absolutely nowhere for them to pee. In the end, they managed to find two empty carrier bags which they soon filled up. The only trouble was finding an escape hatch for the piss bags which, by now, were full to the brim. There were no windows on the coach, of course, and the driver certainly wouldn't open the door for them. So, what they did was to get one of the supporters to open the sky-light for them while they attempted to throw

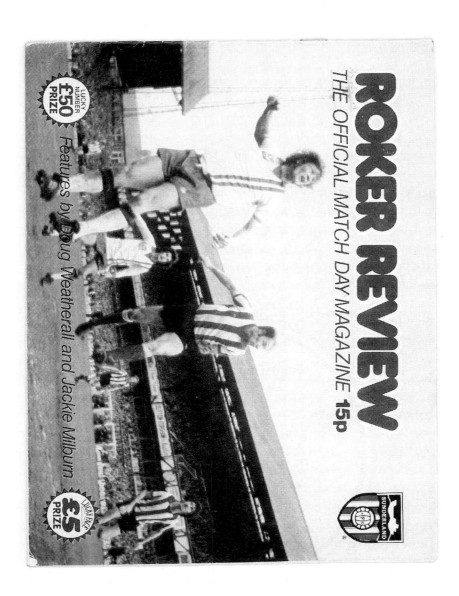

bags out. The sky-light only opened about three inches and every time they tried to squeeze the bags into the opening the contents kept splashing onto anybody within ten feet of it. Every supporter on the back six seats all got soaked with piss, which didn't please anybody, least of all Joy, who, by now, was totally pissed off herself.

We got into the ground and stood in the paddock where the players come out. There were plenty of Liverpudlians scattered around the open terracing behind the goal but because I was with Joy I thought it best to keep away from the scallies, for once. We got talking to this middle aged Sunderland supporter who, during the course of our conversation, was quite happy to extol the virtues of the Liverpool team. On a personal level, you couldn't help but notice his right ear, because it stuck out of the side of his face like Mr. Spock's from the Star Trek series. God help the fella, but it was noticeable that every time he turned to talk your attention was automatically drawn to this ear. I was dying to laugh but Joy

managed to stifle my giggles by kicking my ankle every time I caught breath to speak. The game kicked off and Liverpool were soon in the ascendancy. David Fairclough scored the winner in the 76th minute and suddenly, from being really friendly and appreciative, this Sunderland supporter with the big ear started effing and blinding at us, shouting, 'You jammy bastards, I fucking hate you!' In the end, he stormed off without waiting for the final whistle.

On the coach journey home everybody was happy because we'd won. All the fans were singing and it was a really good atmosphere. Then, out of the blue, this lad who was sitting on the back seat started chanting, 'Whoever's got the biggest tits, get them out.' Seeing as Joy was the only girl on the coach it was quite obvious who his chanting was directed at. Next thing, all his mates shouted, 'Leave it alone will you, you're out of order.' Then one of them said to Joy and me, 'Do you want us to get him for you?' We just said, 'No, leave it, you're alright, mate.' They took no notice because, suddenly, he and his mates grabbed hold of the lad and pulled his trousers down to his knees. One of them went round the coach taking chewing gum off everybody before rolling it into a ball and placing it on the lad's pubic hairs. The poor guy was in agony but everybody else, including us, was in hysterics.

● ● ● ● ● ● ● ● ● ● ● ● ● ●

DARREN PHILLIPS
Journalist

Liverpool v Portsmouth
FA Cup Semi-Final Replay,
Villa Park, April 1992

'Yes, get in, you bastard!' I screamed and joined the thousands of other Reds jumping, dancing and running around the North Bank, as a deli

cately placed John Barnes free kick was palmed away by the Portsmouth keeper to the feet of Ronnie Whelan who fired in from close range. As Ronnie reeled away, arms outstretched to join Barry Venison in hugging Barnsey, and we jigged around a little more I realised that something about all this wasn't right. I shouldn't be reacting like this to a late equaliser against Portsmouth. But this was cup football. Semi-Final cup football at that. If this game had been at Anfield, or even Fratton Park I wouldn't have been as happy about it. I'd want to know why we'd found ourselves in this position for the umpteenth time this season. But it was neither of those places. This was Highbury and we were one step away from the cup final - from the cup itself.

I'd be going to the replay. No doubt about that. I'd followed the cup run each step of the way from Gresty Road to Twerton Park and onto Portman Road and the subsequent replays needed for the latter two games before another trip to Anfield for a quarter final tie against Aston Villa. Our name was on the cup. I knew it if nobody else did. The signs were there. Individual moments of genius apart, no team could have so much luck and not win it. The date for the second game was 13th April with Villa Park as host. Sky TV had the rights to screen the game. It was a Monday evening - not a usual footy night at that time. I had arranged to spend a few days in Blackpool with some mates before we all left college and went our separate ways. We arrived in Blackpool on Saturday night, and were due to leave on Friday morning. I'd checked the train times. Leaving on the 2.45pm to Preston and connecting with the 3.40pm to Birmingham New International,, should get me to the nearby Witton Station around half six that evening. Over an hour to make the ten minute walk to the ground, buy a programme and take in a bit of atmosphere. The train rolled into Preston station around 3.30pm. I found a seat with a table, rolled out my newspaper and waited for the train to depart....and waited, and waited and waited. 'British Rail would like to apologise for the delay of the 15.40 service to Birmingham New International, departing from Platform number four. This is due to essential engineering work. We apologise for this delay,' said a voice from above. No need to worry. I've got an hour to spare. I can still make it. The train eventually chugged out of the station just after five o'clock. Time was going to be tight, very tight. Especially with an unknown connection time from Birmingham to Witton to worry about. In the event the connection was no problem. A train was waiting on the platform and dutifully pulled out minutes after I boarded it. The journey took a little less than ten minutes, but as I caught the train 15 minutes before kick-off I was still struggling to get there on time.

Villa Park's floodlights burned brightly into the night sky as the train stopped. Never having visited the ground and knowing time was against me I decided to take the shortest possible route and headed towards the light. Unfortunately, this meant a patch of wasteland. As I dodged shopping trolleys, planks of wood and half bricks in the twilight, the roar of the crowd increased, I took my eye off the job in hand and ended up thrusting my right foot (not an inconsiderable feat seeing as I take size 13's) down a hole. Finding myself spread-eagled, nose in the dirt before I realised what had happened. Somehow, I managed to negotiate the rest of the rubble without further damage to my already sore ankle and

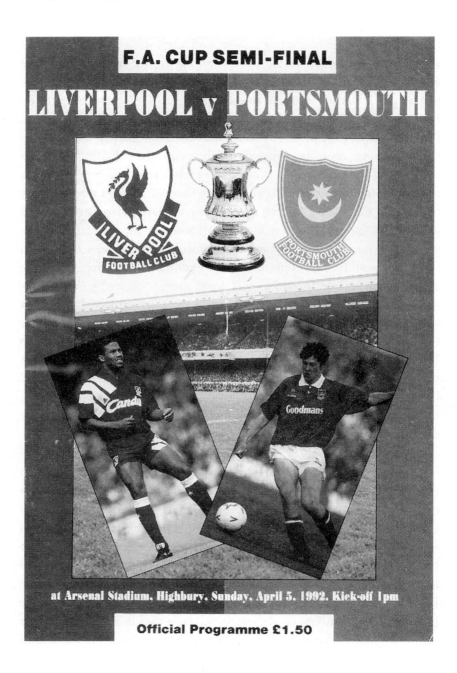

F.A. CUP SEMI-FINAL

LIVERPOOL v PORTSMOUTH

at Arsenal Stadium, Highbury, Sunday, April 5, 1992. Kick-off 1pm

Official Programme £1.50

fortune, and I limped along the remaining streets between me and the ground without further mishap. I then had what appeared to be my first break of the night. A mounted policeman was telling the crowd that kick-off would be delayed to allow everyone a chance to get in. After all that I was going to see the whole match, and took my place on the then Holte End just before the referee tossed the coin.

The subsequent 90 minutes flew by, and were far too close for comfort. Alan McLoughlin hitting the underside of the crossbar straight in front of me, and our seeming inability to defend had me worried, but we survived and caused a few problems of our own. I fancied us to go through in extra time. We have always been the fitter, stronger outfit in the extra period, but the 0-0 scoreline remained. It was down to the dreaded penalties. I was in a confident, if nervous mood as the process began. Experience was bound to help, not to mention Bruce's 'spaghetti legs.' Besides, it was OUR year. I was more sure of that then ever now. Sunderland waited, and despite our inability to see off lower division opposition in 240 minutes of this match, it was as good a chance as any. Three well taken Reds' penalties and poor efforts from Pompey ensured my trip to Wembley.

As the game wore on I knew I'd missed all the connections originally planned for my route back to Blackpool. However, with the likelihood of extra time, I'd checked the timetables for the next set of trains. What I hadn't accounted for was the event of penalties or having the start delayed. Not owning an anorak or having a flask of weak lemon drink about my person I can't claim that my research into BR's timetable was that deep, but I was hoping there would be more. I've never left a match before the last ball has been kicked and I wasn't about to start now. I knew I had to leave almost as soon as the outcome was decided, and yes, that meant marauding across the same waste ground that had claimed my delicate size 13's a few hours earlier. At least the pain had subsided a little. Fortune smiled on me again, as a train waited until it was full of

Liverpool fans before rolling towards central Birmingham. On arrival at New International a tannoy announced that the football special would be leaving for Lime Street in about five minutes. However, my task was to find a train to Preston, or at the very least Wigan, as both would give me a shouting chance of finding my way back to Blackpool and my hotel bed. A departure screen gave me the news I needed. A train for Preston was due to leave at 10.50pm. What time was it now? 10.49pm. 'Where does the Preston train leave from?' I asked the nearest BR employee. 'Just go out of here, and it's the second turning on the right,' he said. 'Thanks,' I bellowed as I disappeared around the corner, took my second right - and saw the train pulling away from the platform. A horn blew, followed by a belch of diesel leaping from the top of the departing locomotive. Just like in a movie cut for TV it masked the expletive embarking from my lips and into the cold night sky. Then I remembered the football special. I could go back to Liverpool. Nobody's going to check my ticket. At the very least I could go home and rejoin the lads in the morning. I retraced my footsteps to the departure board. Platform 12.

Building works were obviously being carried out on the station. White boards hung everywhere covering the walls. It looked like a maze. Another BR guard was collared for directions. At the end of a long corridor I saw a group of Reds running through a gap - that must be the platform. Pain shot through my ankle as I ran. It was the platform, but there was no train. Very few options other than the departure screen presented themselves. On getting there I found that even fewer trains presented themselves, although one was set to depart to Crewe within the half hour. I decided to catch that and just hope that a regional train would be running when I got there. I came through that way so at least there was a chance. Reaching Crewe just before half past midnight I approached a BR guard along with two other people trying to get back from the match, co-incidentally wanting the same information. 'What time is the next train to Preston, mate?' I asked more in dread than hope. The guard hitched up his arm, drew back his sleeve and looked at his watch. A ritual suggesting that a train would be along any time soon. My spirits raised. '.....Ten to eight in't mornin,' lad,' he added then went on his way, leaving me and my two companions - a fellow Red from Warrington and a Portsmouth fan from Wigan open mouthed.

With so much rushing around I'd forgotten how cold it was. My breath billowed out steam. I'd also forgotten how hungry I was. I hadn't eaten since lunch. Crewe, being a busy station, has a 24-hour snack bar - a warm 24-hour snack bar. At least I'd be able to get something to eat. My original plan to have a meal before the game was obviously shelved. Being a vegetarian and very suspicious of consuming anything sold within the confines of a football stadium, I decided to wait until after the game. This was my first chance for a bite to eat. All that remained in the food chiller was a couple of sausage and egg sandwiches. On returning to my new found friends, the Pompey fan, a very nervous and timid looking lad said he was going to find a phone and ring his parents. 'Will they come all this way?' asked the lad from Warrington. 'Oh yeah, they won't leave me here all night,' he said. 'Any chance of a lift?' He hadn't been expecting that. 'Er,.....yeah.....er, no problem,' the poor Wiganer stuttered. He then climbed the stairs to the exit. Disappearing into the night when he reached the summit, never to return. 'That little bastard's fucked off back to Wigan,' said my fellow Red sometime later. By now I'd found out that his name was Ian. 'Probably pissed off because we beat 'em. Wanker! Never had any intention of giving us a lift.' A conclusion I'd reached before he'd left, and didn't really blame him for. After all, who were we? 'Oh well, here for the night then. May as well get some kip,' said Ian as he stretched out across one of the plastic benches. Within minutes he was snoring. I bought a coffee and re-read my newspaper. I've never been the best of rough sleepers, but hoped that the day's exertions would eventually take their toll. Tiredness eventually washed over me. I lay down, closed my eyes and tried to sleep. My eye lids hadn't been closed long before I felt the hard plastic digging against my back. I turned onto my side and felt myself drifting away. Only to be brought back down by the sound of someone mimicking a telephone ringing. Walk around any town, any city and you'll find people out and about who just can't cope with what life had thrown at them, and is still throwing at them thanks to the Government's Care in the Community scheme. In reality, there is no care in the community, just starvation and madness in a gutter. Plus invisibility as society goes about its business and files past. The sight of dishevelled looking people pushing shopping trolleys and looking through bins is so common that it barely raises an eyebrow. Ever thought where these people go at night? In Crewe some head for the warmth and shelter of the 24- hour snack bar at the railway station. I sat up and saw a shabbily dressed man blowing his lips. He let it ring a while longer then said: 'Hello.' Not content with providing his side of the conversation, he decided to change his voice a little and treat us to the voice of the other caller. 'Is Steven there?' he asked himself. 'No, he's out,' he responded. 'Oh, will you tell him that I've got the sausages, and ask him to call me.'.......'No problem, bye.'...'Yeah, see ya.' He put the phone down. Only to pick it up again. 'Ring, ring, ring, ring.' ... 'Hello, it's Steven, you've got the sausages then?' .... 'Yeah, from the butchers, you know - a real bargain.' .... 'I'll come round tomorrow and we'll cook them.' .... 'Tomorrow then?' .... 'Yeah, tomorrow' .... 'Bye' .... 'Bye.' The few people still awake looked away hurriedly. It was three in the morning. There were no more calls, just a three hour monologue of how much he liked sausages. The girl on the snack bar never looked at him, throughout any conversations. Probably all in a night's work. I nearly bought him one of those sausage and egg sandwiches. Not because he probably needed the meal, just to shut him up for a while.

Sleep was impossible, and to keep myself occupied I started to read the foreign news and letters page of the newspaper. I'd had enough of Crewe station to last me a lifetime. I wanted to catch that first train out. I wasn't going to risk missing it. Around six in the morning daylight came, and with it day-time people. The station began to get busy. A newspaper shop opened. I bought some crisps to sate my appetite. Ten minutes before the train was due I woke Ian. 'Quiet night?' he asked. 'Did you get any sleep?' 'Not really,' I replied. 'My back's killing me,' he said. 'That little pie eating nonce better hope we don't play them in a hurry. He doesn't want to bump into me on the Anny Road.'

The seats on the train were comfy. But with this being a through train to Glasgow I didn't want to chance a snooze and end up north of the border. Not with just a few quid in my pocket, which was unlikely to cover the train fare to Blackpool. The conductor came and inspected our tickets. Although mine was a day return, dated yesterday, he chose to say nothing after noticing my red, bloodshot eyes and my sad puppy dog face. He thanked me and walked away. A heart of pure gold. 'Might see you at Wembley,' said Ian as he left the train at Warrington Central. 'I'll definitely be there, so you might just,' I told him. 'I'll organise the travel better, though,' I added. 'Me too,' he said. I got back to our hotel just before eleven. Gave a brief summary of events to the lads before deciding to get some sleep. Accusations abounded. They really thought I copped off with a Brummie girl and stayed the night. I assured them that I couldn't have made that lot up, certainly not when this tired. I collapsed, fully clothed onto the bed, not waking until that evening. Having regained my composure, and while shooting a few games of pool, I reached into my pocket for some change and found a small note from a girl called Karen from Formby asking me to give her a ring. Whether it was the lads winding me up or not I never found out. I'm sorry if you really did see me at the match and took a shine to me Karen, but after a night like that I feared the worst, and decided to cut my losses. I haven't got the bottle, and nice things like that just don't happen to me.

● ● ● ● ● ● ● ● ● ● ● ● ●

JIM GARDINER
Tax Inspector

Arsenal v Liverpool
Caltex Cup
Singapore, May 1991

This game was an end of season jaunt involving ourselves and Arsenal. We travelled direct on tourist class with Singapore Airlines from Manchester airport. It cost us 300 quid but the whole trip was well worth the money. It was a 14 hour flight to the Far East but the long journey was made more than bearable by the standard of service, which was unbe lievable. We were served with two meals and as much drink as we could consume. Anything you wanted was provided by the female cabin staff. Once we arrived in Singapore we were quickly whisked to a smashing hotel which charged £25 per night, which wasn't bad at all considering the luxury of the surroundings. We had full use of the hotel swimming pool, sauna, the lot. Apart from myself, there were three other Liverpudlians in our group and, believe me, we really got looked after by everybody concerned. Talking about the number of supporters who travelled to see the game, I reckon there were roughly ten Liverpool supporters who made the trip though I don't think any Arsenal fans were there. Graeme Souness was the Liverpool manager at the time, of course, but it was Roy Evans who provided us with tickets for the game. We had gone to the hotel where both Liverpool and Arsenal were staying and Roy had handed out tickets to the Liverpool fans who had turned up.

The ground where the match was played was a huge stadium. In fact, it was Singapore's national stadium. It was, quite literally, just a huge all-seated concrete bowl, with no cover to speak of. But a very impressive ground, nonetheless. The only thing that worried me was that Singapore itself suffers from monsoons which normally hit the city around 5pm each day. When the rains fall you certainly get wet, that's for sure! Luckily, it stayed dry for the build-up and duration of the game. The crowd itself was all local people who were visibly excited at the prospect of viewing a game between two of English football's premier clubs. But the interesting thing was, 95% of the crowd were supporting Liverpool on this day. They all had Liverpool shirts on and many of them were cheering on the Reds as vociferously as they do at Anfield.

The game itself ended 1-1 after Arsenal had equalised with about a minute to go. They went on to beat Liverpool on penalties, after that. When the penalties were flying in, or flying wide, as the case may be, the local people were getting really excited but the groans of disappointment after Liverpool had missed their final penalty were noticeable, to say the least.

Probably the highlight of the trip was our frequent trips to a certain bar, which was situated in the centre of town. We would always order the same thing which was a big jug of ice cold Tiger beer and a huge steak sandwich. This would cost us about a fiver, which was really good value. On the night after the game we got chatting to a couple of Dutch lads in this bar and they recommended we pay a visit to a bar called Madigans, which was a pub-cum-nightclub and which was supposed to be the in-place. Quite a few of the Liverpool players did come into the club a little later on to have a drink. Anyway, a group of us were sitting in this bar and two of our lads, Joey Byron from the Wirral, and Phil Antrobus, from Widnes, were getting very friendly with a couple of local girls. The lads were buying them drinks and laughing and joking with the pair. 20 minutes later and I noticed Joey and Phil leaving the club with their arms locked around these two girls. I turned to the two Dutch lads, who had accompanied us, and said, 'Looks like the lads have copped off,' or words to that effect. They said, 'Do your pals know what they're doing?' I replied, 'Oh, don't worry, they're both men of the world. They'll be alright.' But the Dutch guys insisted, 'Do they really know what they're doing?' I asked, 'What do you mean?' And they said, 'Do they really know who they are with?' I was totally confused by now and so I asked them to explain. They told me that the two 'girls' they had left the club with were not really women at all. Apparently, they were women upstairs but downstairs they were most definitely men, if you know what I mean. The two Dutch lads said, 'Perhaps we should warn you're friends?' I laughingly replied, 'No, I think we should let them find out for themselves.' An hour passed then suddenly Joey walked back into the club, stammering, 'You're not going to believe this.......!' Funnily enough, Phil didn't appear for two or three hours and so the jury is still out on him. Thing is, both lads found out the hard way - in more ways than one, I suppose.

JIM GARDINER
Tax Inspector

Glasgow Celtic v Liverpool
Dubai Cup,

The reason I travel to watch Liverpool in these sort of games is purely for the fun and enjoyment of it. Obviously, watching the game is part of it, but, having watched Liverpool in so many of these type of matches I've come to realise they never take them too seriously or try too hard. It's usually treated as a training exercise with the main objective being to get fit and, of course, to avoid any injuries. There is usually a group of us who travel to these type of games, and I'm normally the person who organises the trips. I don't mind because I love sitting down and planning these excursions to foreign countries. On a personal level, I like travelling, anyway, and I use these trips abroad to broaden my horizons and to see places I've never been to before. Yes, I really enjoy it. We always have a laugh and a good bevvy with the lads. As I say, we always treat it purely and simply as a holiday. If I'm going to be blunt, the football itself is only a small part of the trip. Ever since I left school I've never been on a 'proper' holiday. The only holidays I've been on have always involved travelling to watch either Liverpool or Scotland.

The Arabs ran a competition for a number of seasons which was billed as the Championship of Britain. The English champions would play the Scottish champions in a one-off game in Dubai. Liverpool played twice in this competition and on both occasions we played Glasgow Celtic. Everton went out there once and they played Glasgow Rangers, if I recall. The game between Liverpool and Celtic was originally scheduled to be played in December 1988 but because of Liverpool's League Cup commitments the game was cancelled. The game was finally played in April 1989, one week before the Hillsborough disaster.

We flew from London, stopping off at Sofia in Bulgaria, before flying onto Dubai. We were held up in Sofia for about four hours but we sat in the airport bar for the majority of that time, drinking pints of lager at 20p a pint, which wasn't a bad thing. On this particular trip, there were five Liverpool fans, including myself, and, because we'd heard widespread rumours of a no-drinking rule in Dubai, we tried to make up for it in Sofia. We were due to land in Dubai at 4am on the day of the match and were due to leave at 2am the following morning. This schedule didn't leave much room for sightseeing but these things happen, sometimes. Dubai airport is open 24 hours a day and when we arrived in the early hours of the morning we saw people asleep on the airport concourse. We were totally knackered ourselves by this time and so we walked over to the tourist information office to enquire about accommodation for the night. Apparently, there was a hotel which was willing to let us book a couple of rooms for about £40 each. The next problem was, how to get to the hotel? But the tourist information people were really helpful in this respect, because they organised a couple of cars to take us to our hotel. We arrived at 5am and quickly got our heads down for a few hours.

As I mentioned before, we were under the impression that Dubai had a strict non-alcoholic policy but we were wrong. There were nightclubs all over town and the hotel where we stayed had a bar for the residents. It wasn't situated on the ground floor, like most hotels, but on the ninth floor. When we went up there in the lift we found the place full of rich Arabs playing pool and having a bevvy. After a few drinks our group decided to take a walk to the stadium. The stadium itself housed a fabulous sports complex and right next door to this was a big Scottish drinking club, called The Highland Club. Being Scottish myself, I couldn't believe my luck. It was like finding water in the desert. They were selling Tartan special on draught and we quickly made ourselves at home inside the club. We met a few Geordie lads who were working over there and after a few drinks we jumped into their Landrover and went to a nightclub in the centre of town. This was after the game, of course. We really great time but the only thing was we had to catch a flight back in a few hours. If we had known it was so easy to get a drink in Dubai city then we would have stayed for a week. The place was teeming with night-life and the whole atmosphere of the city was awash with excitement. It was a really fabulous place to be in. The nightclub that the Geordie lads took us to was absolutely buzzing and we had a really great time in there.

As I say, there were five Liverpudlians in Dubai to watch the match though, to my knowledge, only one Celtic supporter made the trip over; a guy named Tam McGurran, who I still keep in touch with whenever I'm in Glasgow. We met up with him in the Highland Club and he had a drink with us. As to the match itself, Liverpool were content to use the game merely as a training exercise. Celtic eventually won the game on penalties after both teams had played out a 1-1 draw after 90 minutes. Before the game the Celtic players couldn't believe the behaviour of their English opponents because, the previous evening, the Liverpool team were drinking in the hotel bar until quite late. Both clubs were using the same hotel and, while the Celtic squad were tucked up in bed, our lads were busy downing pints and singing in the bar. The Scottish team were treating this game like a real cup final. To them it was the Championship of Britain, with everything, including pride, at stake. As I say, the Liverpool players were treating the whole trip as a holiday. You couldn't blame them, I suppose, because everything was laid on for them. If they ordered a limousine to take them to an exclusive shop there would be one waiting at the front of the hotel within minutes. If they wanted anything to eat or drink a mountainous tray of food and drink would be served up moments later. Both the Liverpool and Celtic players were treated like royalty for the duration of their stay in Dubai. As for us, we had to leave our hotel to catch the 2am flight out of Dubai, which was a real sickener as we desperately wanted to stay for another few days, at least.

JIMMY THE JOCK
Civil Servant

Liverpool's pre-season tour of Scandinavia, 1990

There were four of us who made this trip. Myself, Phil Antrobus, Joey Byron and Ian Fyffe. All four of us had been to every game on the tour and this was the last match before the Liverpool team flew back for the start of the English soccer season. It had certainly been a long pre-season tour which had started in Paris, moved onto Norway and then finished close to the Arctic circle, which was where we found ourselves for the final game of the tour. Having been away with Liverpool for the best part of two weeks all four of us were fast running out of cash. In fact, we were beginning to panic a little bit because there was very little money left for essentials like food, drink and a hotel room. A couple of the lads managed to alleviate our situation, somewhat, by turning up early at the stadium where the match was being played and coming back with a box of programmes they had managed to find. We knocked them out for 20 Krona, which is about £2, to local supporters who were queuing at the stadium gates. We made about £200 from the sale of the programmes and the first thing we did was to order chicken and chips and a few litres of lager.

I think the game finished in a draw and afterwards we went into town where we ended up in the Sportsman's Bar. One of the lads went up to the bar and ordered four lagers. The barmaid poured the drinks then looked at us, called the manager over and spoke to him. Next thing, she asked, 'Are you boys from Liverpool?' We thought they were going to tell us to drink up and leave, knowing the reputation that Liverpool people sometimes carry with them abroad. I asked outright, 'Why, is there a problem?' The manager replied, 'No problem, these drinks are on the house.' We sat down with our drinks thinking, these people are very socia ble, aren't they! We ordered another four lagers and still they wouldn't take any money from us. A few of the Liverpool players started drifting into the bar then and they were ordering free drinks as well. Then it dawned on us that the management thought we were from Liverpool Football Club. Within the next half hour all the Liverpool players were inside this bar, enjoying their free drinks, while us four went along with the pretence of being part of the club. In the end, Stevie Nicol pulled me aside and said, 'Jim, go and sit over there by Jan Molby and the rest of the lads because they will think you and your mates are with us.' I told him, 'It's alright, Stevie, we've been getting our drinks for nothing, anyway!' The reason for the free drinks policy was because the manager of the bar was so pleased to have the Liverpool players inside his establishment that he was willing to forego payment for the drinks - all night. Mind you, I think he still made plenty of money on the night because the place was absolutely packed out with punters who wanted to rub shoulders with the Liverpool players. The band came on about 10.30pm and by that time I was out of the game. I was rotten drunk. I managed to stagger to the bar to order more drinks and asked the barmaid what time it was. It was 4am and we had been drinking in that bar for almost nine hours without paying for a single drink. The last four people in the bar were myself, Joey Byron, Bruce Grobbelaar and Stevie Nicol. All four of us were in no fit state to stand up but we managed to stagger out of the place a little before daylight.

JIM GARDINER
Tax Inspector

Juventus v Liverpool
European Super Cup
January 1985

Because of other commitments, both Juventus and Liverpool had found it difficult to settle on a date for this game. The original plan was for the match to be played over two legs but eventually it was decided to play a one-off game in Turin, in January 1985, four months before the ill-fated European Cup final, in Brussels.

There were four of us who decided to travel to the game by car. The weather was terrible all the way down to Italy. Maybe for that reason not many Liverpool supporters made the effort to travel over to Turin. There were about 25 fans who travelled over on the official club trip. Apart from that group, ourselves, and two lads who had managed to get to Turin by train, there were no other Liverpool supporters at the game. The Liverpool team arrived in the city the day before the game. Their plane was the only aircraft allowed to land because of the heavy snowfall which had shrouded the whole of Turin. The pitch itself had been cleared just minutes before the game was due to kick off. The snow was piled ten feet high on the touchline. They had used braziers to melt the snow off the pitch in a desperate effort to get the game played.

But the journey itself, for us, was one of the worst journeys to watch Liverpool I can ever remember. Because of the weather conditions none of us wanted to take any of our own cars and so we ordered a cheap hire car. The company wasn't keen on letting any of their vehicles out of the country and so we told them we were planning a short golfing holiday to Inverness, in Scotland. Anyway, we took charge of the vehicle, which was a big Austin Princess and set off for Italy. We drove down to Portsmouth and from there we caught the ferry to Le Havre. Driving through France the weather was atrocious with lorries jack-knifed on the motorway. There was driving snow all the way down through France. We hardly saw any other traffic because the authorities had warned people not to travel - the weather was that bad. Driving down the motorway we saw an endless row of fires which had been lit by stranded lorry drivers as they waited to be rescued.

Two of us took turns at driving but travelling through France we encountered a major problem when the car started breaking down. Luckily, one of the lads, Ian Kendrick, had been in the Royal Engineers and knew how to fix cars. He managed to get the car going again only for it to break down again after we'd gone another 20 miles. This must have happened about ten times, in all. We would have to push-start the car in the middle of a blizzard while he tried to get the engine revving. The temperature outside must have been -10c and it wasn't much warmer inside the car because, unfortunately, the heater had broken down by this time. We kept driving and as the miles passed we were getting closer and closer to Turin. The weather, if anything, was getting gradually worse. But, thankfully, we eventually arrived in Turin in the late afternoon on the day of the game. Passing a school on the outskirts of the city the local school-kids, on seeing our English number plates, started throwing snowballs at us, which we took as being a bit of fun on their part. Entering the centre of town we booked into the first bed and breakfast hotel we came across. After getting something to eat and a change of clothes we travelled over to the team's hotel to try and find Jim Kennefick, the Liverpool FC travel organiser, who had promised us tickets if we made it to Turin. We met up with Jim in the hotel foyer and he boxed us off with our match tickets before arranging for the four of us to travel on one of the two buses which were leaving for the ground in a short while. The players and directors were travelling in the first bus and the press, ourselves and the 25 members who had come on the official trip the second bus. As we travelled through the city towards the stadium both coaches were bombarded with snowballs by Juventus fans. Then they started throwing blocks of ice and apples and oranges at the windows of both coaches. It was getting a bit vicious, to tell the truth. I don't know what the players were thinking but I was certainly getting a bit worried.

The Liverpool fans entered the stadium and once inside were subjected to a barrage of abuse from the Juventus supporters. Out on the pitch, Liverpool played the game in a canter with the result that Juventus strolled the game 2-0. The scoreline could have been a lot worse, to be honest. Platini was pulling the strings in midfield and upfront they had Boniek who literally tore our defence to pieces. Meanwhile, up in the stands, the hatred of the Juventus fans knew no bounds, as they continued to bait us with a barrage of abuse and coins which were continually thrown at us throughout the match. After the game we knew

Liverpool team were flying straight back out. Our plan was to have a night out in Turin before leaving at 5am, the next day, in order to make it back for a league game against Norwich City on Saturday. So, we climbed back on board the coach for the journey back to the team's hotel. By this time all four of us were literally out on our feet, having had very little sleep for almost two days. We knew that the Liverpool players were going onto a reception back at the hotel, before flying out around 12 midnight. And so, we decided to get off the coach and get a taxi back to our guest house. It was the biggest mistake we've ever made because within 100 yards of getting off the coach we were sussed out by a mob of Juventus supporters. We knew they were about to attack us and before they did we carefully manoeuvred ourselves into the middle of the road. Suddenly, all these bricks and bottles started flying toward us. I thought we were going to get battered. But, just as they were about to make their move, Ian, the Royal Engineer, took his life in his hands by jumping in front of this fast taxi, which mercifully stopped before it knocked him down. Ian ran round to the side, opened both doors and shouted at us, 'Get in here, quick!' I shouted at the driver, 'Drive us out of here, mate,!' Thankfully, the taxi driver had his wits about him and he sped off at high speed, putting precious distance between ourselves and the baying mob of Juventus supporters. We never ventured outside that night. Instead, we contented ourselves with a couple of bottles of duty free, which we'd bought on the cross-channel ferry, before setting off for home early the next morning.

In terms of the trouble four months later at the European Cup final in Brussels, I feel that a major contributory factor to the disaster was the behaviour of the Juventus fans in Turin, that night. I know there were only a few Liverpool fans who travelled to the game but word soon spread about the trouble they had encountered over there. Because of that there were a lot of Liverpool fans who were intent on giving the Juventus fans a taste of their own medicine in Brussels. As I say, I'm convinced that the seeds of trouble that occurred at the Heysel stadium were planted by the

Juventus fans in the Stadio Communale, on that cold night in January.

● ● ● ● ● ● ● ● ● ● ● ● ● ●

JIM GARDINER
Tax Inspector

Sunderland v Liverpool
League game, October 1991

It's a sort of tradition with Liverpool, and indeed Everton, for any supporters who travel to these pre-season games to get free tickets off the players and manager. It's different when you're back home, of course, because the players and manager automatically give whatever complimentary tickets they get to family and friends. But for these type of games they normally give their tickets to the ordinary supporters, who have travelled over to watch them. I've got to know Kenny Dalglish, over the years. Basically because we're both from Scotland and because I'm a big lad it's probably been a case of 'once seen never forgotten!' But I've never tried to abuse that friendship by asking for tickets. You just don't do that, do you?

I was in the process of moving house from Worthing in Sussex up to Liverpool around 1991 and amidst all the ballyhoo of moving I'd forgotten to apply for a ticket for the Sunderland v Liverpool game at Roker Park in October of that year. Liverpool had only received about 1,800 tickets, anyway, so it was impossible to find anybody with a spare ticket. I hadn't missed a game for years and so it was obvious I wanted to be at this particular match. As the day of the game drew closer I was beginning to panic. In the end, I had a word with Kenny and, in the process, I explained my predicament. 'No problem, Jim,' he said. 'If you can make it to the team's hotel before 12.30pm I'll see you there. Failing

Normally, I would travel to away games by train with all the lads and we would have a few drinks before catching the last train home. I was so busy sorting the house out, at this time, that I thought my best bet would be to travel to Sunderland by coach and then come straight back to Liverpool after the game. I booked my ticket on the Anfield Travel Club and, after an uneventful journey to the north east, we arrived on the outskirts of Sunderland at 12 noon. I thought, great, time for a few ales before I make my way to the ground. But, the local constabulary still think it's the 1970's up there because they stopped us and kept us waiting for an hour until more Liverpool coaches arrived. They finally escorted the Liverpool convoy to the beach and then let us get off the coach. By the time I finally arrived at the ground it was 2.30 pm and Kenny and the players were already in the dressing room. It was a capacity crowd and there was no way I was going to get into Roker Park to see the game. As a last resort, I sidled up to the ticket office which had a counter which was chest height. Because of its height I had to bend right down to see the person on the other side. I knocked on the window and tried to explain my situation which was that my coach had been held up and I'd missed the chance to pick up my ticket. 'No problem, sir, I'll just check to see if there's an envelope for you,' said the girl behind the counter. 'By the way, what's your name?' she added. 'Jim Gardiner,' I replied. She flicked through the envelopes but couldn't find one with that name on. 'Who left you the ticket,' she asked. 'Kenny Dalglish, the Liverpool manager,' I replied. 'He left a ticket but not for Jim Gardiner,' she said. I thought for a moment and then said, 'Listen love, instead of looking under G for Gardiner, why not look under B for Big Jim.' The girl behind the counter looked at me quizzically, but resumed her search. She suddenly smiled and said, 'Here it is,' before adding, 'how do I know you're Big Jim?' I replied, 'I'll tell you what we're going to do here, Queen. I'll take two steps back from this window and if you will bend your head a little, I think you will be convinced that I'm the man in question.' She took one look and then her hand reached out with this ticket. 'It's yours,' she said.

JIMMY THE JOCK
Civil Servant

Liverpool's pre-season tour of Scandinavia,
Summer 1991

For some reason Kenny always loved to take us to Scandinavia for the pre-season games. We'd travelled all over Sweden and Norway on this particular tour. We had been away for a couple of weeks so money, once again, was tight. We'd saved on our hotel bills by booking overnight travel on trains which had couchettes aboard. They would cost you about a fiver and were well worth it because they allowed you a decent night's sleep because the beds themselves were so comfortable.

The last game of the tour was against HJK Helsinki, who we played in a competitive European game, a few seasons back. It was a cracking journey to Helsinki because we travelled to Stockholm and then caught a ferry to Turku, which is about a two hour train journey from Helsinki. The ferry we travelled on was very luxurious, with bars, a disco, and a cinema. There was plenty of entertainment to keep the passengers, including ourselves, occupied. The journey across the water took 12 hours but because we were able to have a drink on board the ship the journey didn't seem that long. By this stage of the tour the majority of Liverpool fans who had originally travelled had gone home. And so, we were down to six Reds supporters who had stayed on for this final game of the tour. We normally stayed in youth hostels on these pre-season trips and this tour was no exception. The youth hostel we stayed at in Helsinki was part of the football stadium. It was actually situated underneath the main stand which made it handy for the game. We certainly didn't have far to walk, anyway!

As usual, on these pre-season tours, Kenny Dalglish would make it his personal duty that every Liverpool fan who was there was sorted out with tickets. Invariably, he would come up to me and ask, 'How many are here, Jim?' I would tell him and he would hand the tickets over, straightaway. Kenny's testimonial game was due to be played at Anfield the following Tuesday and myself and the other five supporters knew it was going to be tight getting back to Liverpool in time for that game. He said to me, 'Are you going to be back for that, Jim?' I said, 'Of course, Kenny, I'll be there,' before adding, 'just so long as the trains and ferries all leave on time.' He then told me he had a complimentary ticket for his testimonial waiting for me, back at Anfield. As soon as he told me that I began contemplating the long journey home, and the possibilities of making it back to Liverpool in time for the game. Our itinerary meant we had to leave Helsinki first thing in the morning to catch a train back to Turku. We then had to catch the ferry over to Stockholm and then catch the train to Oslo before connecting with the overnight train to Copenhagen. We then had 90 minutes to board our flight to London and then catch the train back to Lime Street. As you can guess, it was two days of non-stop travelling which we had to endure if we wanted to be back in time for Kenny Dalglish's testimonial game. With all this travelling in mind, Kenny asked, 'Why don't you get flights back from Helsinki?' I replied, 'We're all skint, Kenny!' The next thing, the Liverpool manager pulled out all these complimentary tickets for the friendly game and said, 'There's far too many, here.' They were all perforated together and there were so many of them they were falling to the ground in a concertina effect. Kenny asked, 'Can you do anything with these?' before adding, 'you may get a couple of bob for them.' On counting them later, we found there were 35 of these tickets. The price of each was £30 so we knocked them out to the Finnish supporters for £20 apiece, outside the ground. It was so easy. All we did was stop them as they queued up outside the ticket office and offered the tickets to them cheaper. They were snapped up within half an hour. We counted the money and found we had £600 between us. This was great news, because, up to that point, we had been really struggling for money to eat. The two of us who had sold the tickets decided, on a whim, to take advantage of this new situation by purchasing two airline flights next morning which got us into London far earlier than anticipated.

That act of generosity by Kenny was his way of saying, 'Use your loaf, here, lads, and you can fly home, in style.' We were back in Liverpool by Monday tea-time, which was brilliant.

Clutching my complimentary ticket from Kenny Dalglish I made my way to Anfield on Tuesday night and got the best surprise ever. My ticket was, quite literally, the best seat in the house. Thanks to Kenny, I was situated at the front of the director's box, where the opposing manager normally sits. It gave me a grandstand view of the game which I thoroughly enjoyed, courtesy of Kenny Dalglish.

• • • • • • • • • • • • •

KEITH BOYLE
Parts Technician

Brighton & Hove Albion v Liverpool
FA Cup 4th Round Replay
January 30th 1991

I remember walking home from Anfield after the two teams had drawn 2-2 and thinking, 'How am I going to get time off work to go to the replay?' A journey to the south coast would mean explaining to the boss that I needed to take the whole day off work. 'What for?' I imagined him asking. 'To go and watch Liverpool,' I'd reply. 'You can fuck off,' I envisaged him saying. I asked anyway and surprisingly, he just said, 'Go on then, but don't expect to get paid for the time you're taking off.' That was fine by me, and I enjoyed a bit of a lie-in that Wednesday morning before setting off for Lime Street around 11.30am.

A few of the lads had set off earlier that day, having bunked on the ordinary train to London. Myself and two friends, Gary Quayle and Suzy Walker, who was travelling to London to attend a job interview, had railcards which enabled us to travel on the cheap. The train departed just after 12 noon and we whiled away the time by playing cards or reading the newspapers. A lot of the sports writers were doubting Liverpool's ability to survive this hurdle, particularly since Brighton's highly commendable performance at Anfield the previous week. I was always confident we could turn them over on their own turf because they would have to attack more and thus expose themselves to Liverpool's counter-attacks.

We arrived at Euston station and made our way across London to Waterloo station where we caught a connecting train to Brighton. Beforehand, we'd bumped into a few of the lads who had left on the earlier train, including a character called Jimmy Randalls, who was and still is, a complete lunatic, but funny with it, if you know what I mean. This fella normally gets up to all kinds of tricks which are guaranteed to make you laugh. For example, we were in Burger King, in the centre of London and, to ensure he didn't pay for his meal, he suddenly started shouting at the top of his voice, 'Hey, I've been waiting ten minutes for my fucking cheeseburger - where the fucking 'ell is it?' All the girls behind the counter were looking bewildered as none of them could remember serving him. Fact is, they hadn't served him. Jimmy had just stood up and demanded his cheeseburger, even though he'd only just walked into the place. In the end, the manager came over and said, 'Sorry about that, sir, here's your food - and a coke, on the house.' Jimmy's only reply was, 'Nice one, mate!'

We arrived in Brighton in good time for the match and, not having much money on us, we forsook the pleasures of the pub and, instead, went for a walk around the ground. There were about 1,500 Liverpool supporters there. Roughly two-thirds of those were from London and was blowing straight into our faces. Honestly, I've never been so cold at a football match as I was at the Goldstone Ground that night. It was bitterly cold. I couldn't wait for the match to end so we could get back onto the train and get warm. Of course, the game itself went into extra time, which meant another 30 minutes standing on that open terrace.

But before the game there had been a bit of trouble between the Brighton touts and the Liverpool scallies. Apparently, the Liverpool lads had given the local touts a lesson in how to operate. As usual, Jimmy Randalls was involved as he had sold tickets to two Brighton supporters for 20 quid apiece. 'Yeah, they will get you into the main stand,' he'd answered, when asked what part of the ground these tickets were for. As soon as the sale had been made Jimmy scarpered. I asked his mate why he'd suddenly done a runner? 'Because he's just sold them two fucking car-park tickets, that's why!' The touts from Brighton accused the Scousers of ripping everybody off. Mind you, they were ripping everybody off, as well. It was just that the Sussex lads weren't as wise to the scams that the Liverpool lads were up to.

As soon as the final whistle went after we'd beaten Brighton 3-2 the majority of Liverpool supporters ran onto the pitch. It was more to keep warm than to celebrate. I remember touching John Barnes's arm and all I could hear him saying, was, 'Come on lads, get off the pitch.' Eventually, the Liverpool supporters climbed back onto the terraces and made their way back to their transport. A gang of us travelled back on the first available train from Brighton to Waterloo. Up to now, there had been very little trouble but that almost changed on the journey from Waterloo to Euston on the London underground. Jimmy had been staring out a gang of black guys who were standing on the platform. Now, I'm not saying that Jimmy is a hard-case. To tell the truth, he's a bit of a shit-house, really. That's why he made sure the train was moving before he put his hands under his shoulder blades in a monkey impersonation. He thought he was really funny until this huge black guy, who, unbeknown to Jimmy, gotten on the train and sat next to me. Jimmy turned round, laughing, and saw this 6ft 7in black fella looking straight at him, saying, 'You offended me, man.' Jimmy's face went the colour of boiled shite. But, he managed to blurt out, 'Yes, but, they were slagging me off, you know what I mean.' The black fella repeated, 'I don't care, you offended me, man.' By this stage, Jimmy was nearly crying but luckily the next stop was Euston and as soon as the train stopped he quickly jumped off and scarpered up the escalator before the fella could grab hold of him.

We had 30 minutes to wait before the Liverpool train left and in the meantime we got talking to a woman who was travelling back from London. She was about 45 years of age, but looked older. She was a Scouser and she was happy to talk to the Liverpool fans on the station concourse. We ended up sharing a carriage with her all the way home. When the train got going she pulled out this bottle of vodka with a bottle of bitter lemon to accompany it. Jimmy, on seeing this, saw the opportunity of some serious piss-taking. The woman herself began effing and blinding after she'd had a few drinks. Jimmy was shouting all over the carriage, 'Fuck off, you drunken bastard.' She was shouting back, 'I'll fucking kill yer, if I get my hands on you, yer bastard.' Next thing, she threw a bottle of coke at Jimmy, but he managed to dodge it and it hit the window with a crash. 'Never touched me!' Jimmy taunted her. A couple of minutes later the woman decided she needed to go to the toilet and one of the lads, Steve Christie, thinking he was on for something, went with her. She was gone for about 15 minutes and, in the meantime, Jimmy had grabbed the bottle of vodka and bitter lemon which he proceeded to piss into, before carefully placing it back onto her table. We were protesting, 'You can't let her drink it.' But then we thought, 'Oh, fuck it, it'll be a laugh.'

When the woman came back with Steve he started boasting to the rest of the lads that she had just sorted him out with a wank in the mail-carriage. None of us believed a word of what he was telling us, of course.

The woman was oblivious of all this talk because as soon as she sat down she picked up her bottle of vodka and bitter lemon and swigged it. We waited with bated breath for the nauseating scream......which never came! She was obviously too far gone to notice or to care by that time. We shared a taxi with her at Lime Street and dropped her safely home. It was the least we could do after the fun she had inadvertently given us that night.

● ● ● ● ● ● ● ● ● ● ● ● ●

TERRY COTEY
Student Teacher

Arsenal v Liverpool
League game, September 1984

This was my first proper away game. My brother, Eddie, had taken me to watch Liverpool play Arsenal in the Charity Shield game at Wembley in 1979, which the Reds had won by three goals to one. I was only 11 at that time so was far too young to be going to away games on my own. We absolutely annihilated the Gunners that day and I really enjoyed the occasion. It certainly whetted my appetite for travelling to see Liverpool. Five years later and I was considered old enough to go and watch them away from home. A group of friends and I set off from Lime Street on the ordinary train, full of anticipation of what the day held in store. Being young and probably naive I was rather in awe of travelling to London. I'd heard all the stories of trouble which my older brothers had encountered down there, over the years. This only served to excite me even more. The prospect of coming face to face with Arsenal's mob certainly got the adrenalin going. There were a lot of older Liverpool supporters on our train. By old, I mean fellas who must have been around 25 years of age. It was obvious they were old hands at this game. Listening to their conversations on the journey to Euston I was struck by their apparent gard for the 'enemy.' When we reached London there was a large police presence waiting to escort the Liverpool fans to their underground train. Walking across the concourse of Euston station you could see small pockets of Arsenal supporters eyeing up our mob, which, incidentally, was about 200 strong. There wasn't any trouble though one or two of the Arsenal supporters were baiting us with shouts of, 'Scouse wankers!' It would have been easy to break away from the escort and attack the cockneys but no sooner would you have done so then the police would have nicked you. We reached Highbury station and walked through a park toward the ground. There was still no sign of any Arsenal mob. We continued walking until we reached the stadium itself. It was then the first signs of trouble erupted as a mob of around 300 Arsenal fans converged on our patch, by the Clock end of the ground. Liverpool's mob, which had grown to around 500 by now didn't chicken out. On the contrary, they chased the Arsenal mob down toward the Northbank. The police moved in then and everybody scattered. On a personal level, I thought this was great sport because, so far, Liverpool were ruling the roost round Highbury. It was just a pity the team couldn't do the same inside the ground because Arsenal tore us apart, beating us 3-1. Only a late Ray Kennedy goal saved Liverpool from a complete whitewash. Coming out of Highbury we made sure the Liverpool mob stayed together. 'Come on, let's go round to their end,' one nutter shouted. As things turned out, we didn't need to because Arsenal came looking for us instead. The subsequent pitched battle was frightening but exciting at the same time. I was a mere novice when it came to stuff like this but I didn't allow my inexperience to intimidate me at all. Liverpool had a good mob with them that day and it served us well because we were able to hold our own to such an extent that Arsenal's mob were beaten back by the sheer ferocity of our fighting. As the police, once again, moved in to quell the disorder the Liverpool mob moved swiftly away from the scene. Instead of travelling back to Euston by underground we decided to make the journey on foot. Half an hour later and we found ourselves close to Kings Cross station. That's when we bumped into a mob of around 25 Chelsea porters on the road which leads from Kings Cross to Euston. We battled with them for a while and then made our way back to Euston station. Once there, we encountered a large group of Birmingham City supporters, who had been to watch their team play Crystal Palace. There were more scuffles involving these before the Brummies were forced onto their train by the police. We finally made it onto the Liverpool train at around 6.30pm, tired but elated at the day's events.

● ● ● ● ● ● ● ● ● ● ● ● ● ● ●

STAN BOARDMAN
Comedian

Liverpool v Arsenal
FA Cup Final, May 1971

I first attended Anfield when I was six when my dad took me onto the Kop. I wouldn't mind but he made me stand right in the middle of the terraces - which was pretty scary for a young lad. He did make some allowance by wrapping his coat around one of the crush barriers, which I then sat on. All the people around would protect the kids and it always amused me that anybody who fainted would get passed down from the top of the Kop to the bottom and into the waiting arms of the St. John Ambulance people; because it seemed to me that they would have the best view of the game.

I've been all over Britain and Europe following Liverpool. That was when I was younger, of course. These days I'm so busy I hardly have time to go and watch the Reds. Mind you, at one time I wouldn't even think about taking a booking for a show if the date clashed with a Liverpool match. Because of work commitments I do have to pick and choose my games a little, these days.

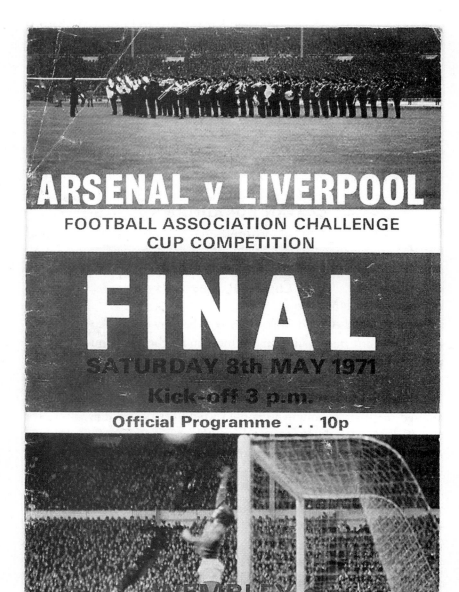

ARSENAL v LIVERPOOL

FOOTBALL ASSOCIATION CHALLENGE
CUP COMPETITION

FINAL

SATURDAY 8th MAY 1971

Kick-off 3 p.m.

Official Programme . . . 10p

Empire WEMBLEY Stadium

But if we're talking about away games, one of the best trips I ever went on was to the 1971 FA Cup final against Arsenal. We travelled down to London in this battered old mini. The car wasn't working very well and eventually it broke down a few miles from our destination. This was 11 o'clock in the morning. We weren't far from Wembley but because none of us had tickets for the game we were keen to get to the ground early to try and find a place to bunk in. Luckily enough, the hotel that the Liverpool players were staying at was only a few minutes walk away and so my mates and I decided to walk over and see if we could meet the players. When we arrived at the hotel there were loads of security guards keeping watch over the entrance gates. Seeing this, my mates and I walked round to the side of the building and promptly climbed over the wall - jumping, commando style, amongst the bushes on the other side. We stealthily crept along the herbaceous borders until we happened upon the side entrance to the hotel. We walked into the building as if we were paying guests and nobody challenged us, which was great. We sat down in the hotel foyer then and promptly ordered a pot of tea between us. When the waitress brought our drinks she looked at us knowingly, but didn't say anything. Don't forget, we were dressed from head to foot in red and white and must have looked a little out of place in this big posh hotel. To avoid getting caught we took our tea on the lawn. Five minutes later we were sitting there when Bill Shankly came walking down the steps toward us, along with Rueben Bennett, the coach. The first words out of his mouth were, 'Alright, lads, how are you doing?' It was brilliant. There we were taking tea on the lawn of the player's hotel and talking to the great Bill Shankly. After a few minutes he asked if we were alright for tickets for the game? 'None of us have got tickets, Bill,' I answered. 'Don't worry, son, I've got a few spare tickets here,' he replied. Next thing, the Liverpool manager pulls out four tickets and hands them to me. 'Here you are. Enjoy the game, son,' he said. My three mates and I couldn't thank him enough for his gesture. We offered to pay for the tickets, saying, 'How much do we owe you, Bill.' He replied, 'Och, son, you take them, you deserve them.'

LIVERPOOL F.C.   SEASON 1970-71

BACK ROW (left to right): Peter Thompson, Alec Lindsay, Ray Clemence, Tommy Lawrence, Chris Lawler, Ian Ross. MIDDLE ROW: Alun Evans, John McLaughlin, Larry Lloyd, John Toshack, Steve Heighway, Phil Boersma, Brian Hall. FRONT ROW: Bobby Graham, Emlyn Hughes, Ron Yeats, Mr. W. Shankly, (Manager), Tommy Smith (Captain), Ian Callaghan, R. Paisley, (Trainer).

ARSENAL		LIVERPOOL
(Yellow Shirts, Blue Shorts, Yellow Stockings)		(Red Shirts, Red Shorts, Red Stockings)
1. R. WILSON	Extra Time	1. R. CLEMENCE
2. P. RICE		2. C. LAWLER
3. R. McNAB		3. A. LINDSAY
4. P. STOREY	REFEREE	4. T. SMITH (Captain)
5. F. McLINTOCK (Captain)	NORMAN BURTENSHAW	5. L. LLOYD
6. P. SIMPSON	(Great Yarmouth, Norfolk)	6. E. HUGHES
7. G. ARMSTRONG		7. I. CALLAGHAN
8. G. GRAHAM		8. A. EVANS
9. J. RADFORD		9. S. HEIGHWAY
10. R. KENNEDY	LINESMEN	10. J. TOSHACK
11. C. GEORGE	G. C. Kew (Leeds)	11. B. HALL
Substitute: J. SAMMELS	J. Bell (Newcastle)	Substitute:
Manager: Mr. B. MEE		Manager: Mr. W. SHANKLY
Trainer: Mr. G. WRIGHT		Trainer: Mr. R. PAISLEY

RESULTS . . . SCORERS . . . ON THE WAY TO WEMBLEY

ARSENAL		LIVERPOOL	
Third Round Yeovil Town (Away) (Radford 2, Kennedy)	3-0	Third Round Aldershot (Home) (McLaughlin)	1-0
Fourth Round Portsmouth (Away) (Storey, penalty)	1-1	Fourth Round Swansea City (Home) (Toshack, St. John, Lawler)	3-0
Fourth Round Portsmouth (Home) (George, Simpson, Storey, penalty) (Replay)	3-2	Fifth Round Southampton (Home) (Lawler)	1-0
Fifth Round Manchester City (Away) (George 2)	2-1	Sixth Round Tottenham Hotspur (Home)	0-0
Sixth Round Leicester City (Away)	0-0	Sixth Round Tottenham Hotspur (Away) (Heighway)	1-0
Sixth Round Leicester City (Home) (George) (Replay)	1-0	(Replay)	
Semi-final Stoke City (Hillsborough, Sheffield) (Storey 2,1 penalty)	2-2	Semi-final Everton (Old Trafford, Manchester) (Evans, Hall)	2-1
Semi-final Stoke City (Villa Park, Birmingham) (Replay) (Graham, Kennedy)	2-0		

We told Bill about our car breaking down and he said, 'Don't worry about that, son - the four of you can come with us to the game.' An hour later, all four of us were sitting on the second coach which was reserved for the player's wives. We couldn't believe our luck. When we eventually set off from the hotel all the staff came out to wave us off and my mates and I were waving back at them, thinking, 'This is great, isn't it?' That was nothing compared to the welcome we received along Wembley Way. There were thousands of fans all lined up on the pavements cheering the coach. I know they were cheering the occupants of the first coach but we made sure they noticed us four. We were banging on the windows and waving our scarves at the Liverpool supporters outside. They must have thought, 'Who are they?' before concluding that we must be reserves.

We got into the ground using the tickets Bill Shankly had kindly given to us and watched the match. We were sick at getting beat but were still in good heart at the thought of a good night out in London that evening. My mates and I were never ones to do anything by half and so we decided to try and bunk into the Savoy Hotel in the centre of London. We knew that's where the post-match banquet was being held and were determined to be there. It wasn't that difficult to get past the flunky on the door as we told him we were reserve team players. I was nearly telling the truth, as well, because when I was a kid I was on Liverpool's books. I played a few times for the A & B teams but never quite made it into the reserve side. I eventually left the club a year before Bill Shankly arrived. Who knows, I might have made it if I'd still been there after the great man took over as manager. But anyway, there we were in the grand ballroom of the Savoy, with all the players and their wives. Sid Reakes, the former Liverpool director, and Matt Busby were just leaving their table and so we glided over to where they had been sitting, saying to them, 'Are these seats finished with, Matt?' The Manchester United manager replied, 'Help yourself, son.' Bill Shankly was standing a couple of feet away and he gave us the thumbs-up sign and smiled at us. It was a good party but everybody was on a bit of a downer because we'd been beaten by Arsenal.

My mates and I got drunk and tried to forget about the result. We ended up talking to all the players and their wives. It turned into a really good night which everybody enjoyed.

● ● ● ● ● ● ● ● ● ● ● ● ● ●

ALAN PARRY
Sports Commentator

Benfica v Liverpool
European Cup Quarter Final, 1st Leg
Lisbon, March 1978

I was working for BBC Radio Merseyside at the time and our bosses at the BBC, in their wisdom, sent Eddie Hemmings and me over to Portugal to report on Benfica v Liverpool in the European Cup quarter final. As a red-hot Liverpudlian, it's fair to say I was over the moon to be given this particular assignment. We arrived in Portugal in good time for the game as well as a bit of sightseeing in the daytime. On the day of the game, though, the heavens opened........and stayed open, all day and night. Honestly, it never stopped raining for hours and hours. By the time we arrived at the ground we were already soaked to the skin. Our notes were soaked - everything was wet through. And all because neither of us thought to bring an umbrella. But we quickly made ourselves comfortable in the Benfica press-box, which is right opposite that vast bank of terracing which is a feature of the Stadium of Light. We telephoned London to check that all our equipment was working. Thankfully, everything was and we relaxed enough to drink a cup of coffee which we'd managed to secure from the press-room before taking our seats. As the two teams arrived on the pitch the Benfica supporters, en masse, stood up to see the events. Being aware of the conditions the same fans had also come fully prepared, as everyone of them was carrying an umbrella.

Because of this, neither Eddie nor I could see a blade of grass. We weren't worried at that stage because we both thought that once the game kicked off the fans would sit down. Trouble was, they continued to stand when the referee blew his whistle to start the game. By this stage, neither of us could do anything but guess at what was happening out on the pitch. Our connection in London was screaming frantically down the wire, 'What's happening, Alan?' I had to tell the truth. 'I don't honestly know......I can't see a thing for all these umbrellas.'

Eventually, Eddie and I had the idea of extending the microphone cable into the crowd which meant reporting on the game from outside the press-box. This meant clambering over a soaking wet wall - negotiating a fairly big drop (mindful all the time of landing on top of a Benfica supporters head) and then climbing over occupied seats before taking our place on the steps which led to the back of the stand. All the while the Benfica supporters, knowing we were English, kept up this barrage of noise, which was purely designed to put us off our commentary.

After a while a middle-aged Benfica supporter climbed out of his seat and suddenly grabbed the microphone out of my hand and started shouting, 'Benfica, Benfica,' down the line. I don't know what the BBC crew back in London must have thought at that point, but I know what I was thinking, and it certainly wasn't meant for family listening, I can tell you! This was a live transmission, don't forget, and because of this the guys in London were screaming, 'Can't you shut him up?' I pleaded with the Benfica supporter to go away but unfortunately he wouldn't. In the end, I got all my spare Escudo's out of my pocket and offered them to him, in the hope that this would shut him up. It was my biggest mistake. You would think I'd insulted his mother, grandmother, son and daughter all at once, because he suddenly went absolutely crazy. He was ranting and raving like a madman. For a moment I thought I was going to be attacked but, luckily for me, he calmed down enough to return to his seat. Next thing, Emlyn Hughes scored and all hell let loose around me. As the ball hit the net I jumped up and shouted down the microphone, have scored. Emlyn Hughes has put the Reds in front with a blistering shot from 20 yards.' The Liverpool fans back home must have been jumping with glee at that point. To be honest, I was just as gleeful but my celebrations were soon brought down to earth with a bump by my erstwhile Benfica chum who suddenly came from behind before walloping me so hard on the back that I fell headlong into the crowd - almost swallowing the microphone in the process! I was desperately trying to keep up appearances by continuing my commentary but it was impossible because, by this stage, I was crawling among feet, knees and elbows, in a frenzied effort to locate the microphone. I suddenly heard a crackling BBC voice, saying, 'We seem to have lost Alan Parry, for the moment.' If the situation wasn't so serious one might have laughed at the absurdity of it all.

Eventually I managed to find the microphone and continue the commentary. Thankfully, my back-slapping friend didn't bother me again and I was able to report a famous Liverpool victory. Despite all that went on, it was still one of the most enjoyable - and with hindsight - one of the funniest trips I've had following Liverpool Football Club.

EDDIE COTTON
Author

Newcastle Utd v Liverpool
League game, St. James Park
&
Crusaders v Liverpool
European Cup, 1st Round, 2nd Leg
Belfast
September 1976

A special train left Lime Street, bound for Newcastle's Manor Park station at 9.30am on Saturday morning. The train, which would normally carry 500 fans was nowhere near full for this particular game. Only 350 brave souls had ventured from Liverpool to see the Reds in action. The probable reason for so few Liverpool fans making the trip was because Newcastle was never classed as a city you would care to visit in a hurry. And especially so when the home side were playing your own team. The Geordie's, in those days, had a reputation for savagery, which was perhaps matched only by West Ham's ICF crew, in London or Manchester United's Red Army. The small number of Liverpool supporters who made this trip knew what to expect later that afternoon but, like me, they put all thoughts of trouble to one side as they duly began to open their obligatory cans of lager.

As the train suddenly lurched out of Lime Street station on that cold but sunny autumn morning I realised that the next four days would certainly sort the real Liverpool supporters from the part-time variety. In two days hence, I would be one of the foolish few making the trip over to Belfast to watch Liverpool take on Irish part-timers Crusaders in the European Cup, first round, second leg tie, which was to be played on Tuesday afternoon. The possibilities of receiving a good kicking by Newcastle United's finest was but a passing concern when compared to

EUROPEAN CHAMPIONS CUP
1st Round - 2nd Leg

CRUSADERS v LIVERPOOL

SEAVIEW, TUESDAY, 28th SEPTEMBER

KICK-OFF 4 p.m.

Price 15p

the potentially life threatening journey to Belfast next week.

'Hope we don't fucking win, today,' exclaimed Billy Weaver, who normally would be the life and soul of any away trip. We all laughed along at his jokey assertion, but the lads knew precisely what he meant because we fully expected a crew to be waiting as soon as our train arrived in the north east. Looking around our carriage, which housed 50 of Liverpool FC's top boys, you couldn't help but be impressed at the lack of concern and general joviality which pervaded the carriage throughout the long journey to Newcastle. Card schools were commenced, cans of lager were drank and what food people had was consumed with a vigour which seemed to undermine any cause for concern we felt for the forthcoming confrontation with the Geordie's.

Approximately three hours after leaving the safety of Lime Street we began to near Newcastle. The suburbs of the city flew by as the bridge across the River Tyne approached rapidly. Looking out of the window I spied the nearby hustle and bustle of the Saturday shoppers, going about their lawful business. A pity, I thought, that the vast number of local hooligans who were already waiting for us at Manor Park station couldn't accompany their own mothers on a day like today. But, I suppose, silly thoughts like that were girlish in the extreme. Especially so when I looked around and witnessed the other 49 occupants of the carriage arming themselves, both mentally and physically, for the ensuing battle of St. James Park. 'Come on, lads, whatever happens, we've got to stick together,' was my friend, John Gargan's cry as the train finally came to a halt. At most other grounds it would be laugh and joke time, at this point, but not today. Put it this way, nobody was exactly rushing for the door of the carriage. As the Liverpool supporters, all 350 of us, stepped onto the platform one could see nervous glances all around you. Somebody at the front of the mob shouted, 'Give us an L,' but nobody sang 'L,' and that was the end of that particular chant. I was hoping nobody would dare to sing, 'Those were the days,' because its lyrics included the life threatening line, 'We fucked the Geordie's too, we are the Kop of Liverpool FC.' Nobody did, thank goodness, and we walked out of the station to be confronted by a mob of around 100 Geordie's, dressed in the black and white stripes of their team. 'Come 'ed,' shouted a big Scouser at the front and everybody tensed. 'Come 'ed, they're shithouses,' the same fella shouted and with that we ran at their mob. They stood their ground for about ten seconds and then chose to run away. We chased them across the railed flyover which separated the station from the main part of the city centre. At first we didn't think we would catch up but gradually our mob gained on them as the flyover suddenly narrowed into steps on the other side of the road. Fists and boots flew in wicked abandon as the Scousers laid siege on the Geordie boys. In their haste to escape, the Newcastle mob were jumping over the railings into the street below, which was a drop of about 15 feet. Some weren't so quick on their feet and they got the shit kicked out of them by the Liverpool crew. With confidence high from this initial sortie, the Liverpool mob gradually made their way into the centre of Newcastle. For the first time since arriving in the city our mob began to make some sort of noise. 'Liverpool, Liverpool,' we sang with confident abandon. The Saturday shoppers, both young and old, looked warily at us. I was at the front of the mob by this time and glancing back to see how far back we stretched I was struck by how big our mob actually looked. As we snaked our way through their city centre we began to see small groups of Newcastle boys on each corner, looking over at us. They were obviously sizing up the opposition. We didn't bother to get involved with fighting any of these small gangs as our main purpose was to arrive at St. James Park in strength, thus impressing the local supporters, who we knew would be queuing outside the ground in large numbers, waiting for the gates to open.

'The Reds are coming up the hill, boys.......!' became our refrain as we finally arrived outside the Gallowgate end of the ground. As expected, there were hundreds of Newcastle fans waiting patiently for the gates to open but, not surprisingly, none of them made a move to attack us. I was confident they wouldn't anyway, because you could see they were merely 'football fans' as opposed to 'football thugs.' As the gates finally opened we decided to make our way into the ground. One or two of the more foolhardy members of the Liverpool mob shouted, 'Let's go round to their end.' Let's not push our luck, I thought, when that particular idea was suggested.

CRUSADERS—THE IRISH LEAGUE CHAMPIONS—front row (left to right)— Bobby McQuillan, Jeff Gorman, Billy Johnston (Manager), Derek Wade (Chairman), Walter McFarland, Joe McKee (President), George Lennox, Drew Cooke, Robert Strain.
Second Row—Harry Megaw (trainer), Ronnie McAteer, Robert Gillespie, Roy McDonald, John McPolin, Paul Kirk, Johnny Wallace, Dick Sterritt.
Back Row—Wallace McIlveen, George Wilton, Jack Sloan, Jim Bruce, Harry McClelland, George Bruce, Jimmy Miller, Shaflo McCrea.
The trophies are—Player of the Year—Jeff Gorman, Irish Cup and Good Conduct Trophy awarded by the N.I. Professional Footballers Association.

In those days the home supporters were mostly congregated in the Leazes end of the ground which was directly opposite our position in the open Gallowgate end. Mind you, the Newcastle mob was so strong they could afford to lose 500 of their number from the home end. These mindless morons usually situated themselves in the away end of the ground. Today was no exception, of course. As kick-off time approached one could see large groups of Newcastle boys gathering in various parts of the terracing, looking our mob up and down. A shiver ran down my spine as I contemplated the pitched battle that could start at any moment. But that particular fear was distinguished by the sudden arrival of the local constabulary, who surrounded our mob on all sides. As the game kicked-off both crews momentarily forgot about fighting and chas ing and running as all eyes quickly settled on the events taking place on the pitch.

Newcastle played well - Liverpool played averagely. The final result probably reflected the whole 90 minutes as the home side grabbed the spoils with the only goal of the game. The Newcastle supporters were in raptures, and I didn't blame them as their team had truly deserved their victory on the day. As the full-time whistle blew I remembered Billy Weaver's words that morning: 'Hope we get beat!' he'd said. Well, we had been beaten but looking at their departing mob there was little to suggest they had comradeship in mind. 'You're gonna get your fucking heads kicked in,' they sang with gusto. As our mob prepared itself for the inevitable street battle which we knew would take place as soon as we stepped into the dimly lit streets which surrounded St. James Park, the police suddenly began to move away from us. This prompted somebody to ask, 'Can we have an escort to the station?' A big sergeant gruffly replied, 'Fuck off you Scouse bastards, you can look after yourselves.' And so, rather like General Custer in the Battle of the Little Big Horn, we embarked on a journey into, what I personally termed, Indian country. Picture the scene for yourselves. It was raining - it was dark - it was cold - it was fucking scary! There were mobs of Newcastle everywhere. And I mean EVERYWHERE. They were up street lamps, down grids, in shop doorways, underneath parked cars. Everywhere you looked you found yourself staring at a black and white nightmare. What would you do in a situation like that? All we could do was either stick together or try and get lost in the crowd. Guess what? We elected to get lost in the crowd. Things became a blur at that point because I closed my eyes and thought of stabbing myself so their mob would take pity on me. It was a stupid thought, I know, but you can't help thinking stupidly in times of great stress. Instead, in an effort to look nonchalant and cool I began to sing. My dearest wish was that any potential assailant would come to the conclusion that anybody cocky enough to be singing Rod Stewart's You Wear It Well, while walking home from the match must be a home

I'd covered most of Rod Stewart's greatest hits before disaster struck on the flyover which led to Manor Park station. I was a mere 100 yards from safety when a group of Newcastle's finest suddenly realised I was a Scouser. 'What time, is it, mate?' they asked in an absurdly polite fashion. I was tempted to say, 'Time you got a watch, you Geordie bastard,' but I didn't want to upset them. 'He's a Scouser, get him,' one of their number shouted. A punch flew straight into my face - and another, before somebody came from behind and punched me in the shoulder. I went down like a bag of shite and the boots began to rain down on my prone body in unmerciful fashion. I rolled into a ball and wondered if I'd make it to Belfast if this beating carried on much longer. Thankfully, one of them shouted, 'Leave him, he's had enough!' I felt like replying, 'You can say that again!' but I thought it wise to pretend I was dead, at that moment.

Having picked myself up from the cold, wet floor I limped the remaining 100 yards to the station. The attack had been witnessed by the vast majority of the Liverpool mob, who had miraculously made it back to safety. 'Are you alright, Eddie?' somebody asked with a concerned air. 'I'm okay,' I replied. Billy Weaver pointed to my eye, exclaiming, 'Have you seen the black eye, you've got?' Realising I had a shiner cheered me up considerably. 'What's it like?' I asked. 'It looks good, mate!' John Gargan replied.

Two nights later I found myself clearing customs along with 50 other Liverpool supporters as we boarded the Liverpool to Belfast ferry at Princes Dock, near to the Pier Head. My black eye had become the prominent feature of my face in the intervening 48 hours. Everybody I met asked how I'd received it and I proudly told them. 'I got it at Newcastle last Saturday.' This is purely a personal aside, but I can't help thinking how absurd it is to be young and impressionable enough to believe that a black eye would open all kinds of possibilities, including the chance to impress both your mates and, of course, girls. Amazingly, jumped off the 12 bus in James Street, when two girls stopped me and asked for a light. 'I don't smoke,' I replied. 'Where are you going?' the older one queried. I told her and she asked could she walk down to Princes Dock with me. 'Come on then,' I said. 'What's your name?' she asked. 'Eddie. What's yours?' I asked in return. 'I'm Kim and this is Jackie,' she answered. We talked as we walked and Kim even linked me as we approached Princes Dock. Unfortunately, in those days I was a shy boy and I didn't have the nerve to try and get my grips, which, in hindsight, I should have done. But I did kiss her, or rather, she kissed me just before we arrived at the Dock. All my mates, waiting at the entrance hall, whistled in appreciation of the romanticism of the moment. One or two of them asked, 'Who's she, when she's out?' I replied, 'Oh, just somebody I met by the Pier Head.'

Having witnessed my pre-sailing necking session with Kim they must have presumed that I was some kind of boss shagger. I didn't crack on that I was still a virgin, at the time. But you don't, do you, when you're young.

Having cleared the beady eyes of customs, who, thankfully, were able to distinguish our mob from a gang of IRA terrorists, we boarded the Belfast ship and quickly made ourselves at home in the bar. I didn't drink but the older Liverpool supporters began to order pints of bitter and lager. Five miles out from the Mersey Bar and the drinking lounge was awash with fans as well as ordinary passengers singing Liverpool FC songs. The atmosphere was brilliant, with everybody having a good time. My friend, Billy Hignett, from Norris Green, and myself went walkabout around the decks of the ship, mainly on the lookout for girls we could chat up. We found some too. Jean and Carol, who, it turned out, lived on the Shankill Road. Billy and I, being Catholics, thought it wise not to bring up the subject of religion. It would only have got in the way of the sugar candy kisses we received from the two Protestant girls. After we'd got our grips on the lower deck, Billy, in mischievous mood, asked Carol, 'How is King Billy, these days?' Luckily, they saw the funny side and after a brief respite for air all four of us resumed our necking session as the wind from the Irish Sea blew waves along the decks of the ship.

Many hours later, Billy and I, having kissed the girls goodnight, made ready to set foot onto Irish soil. All the Liverpool fans present looked understandably nervous. Couldn't blame them really as the troubles were at their height in 1976. My way of thinking was simply that politics and religion shouldn't get in the way of a good football match. I was fervently praying the locals felt the same way. 20 minutes after disembarking from the ship, Billy and I were joined by a lad we knew vaguely from the match. I forget his name but he invited us both to accompany him and his two friends, who were from Belfast, to their house which, it turned out, was on the outskirts of the city. We shook hands with the two fellas, who were called John Sweeney and Billy Crabtree. They both had beards and red hair, which they wore long. Both were about 25 years of age. They greeted us by saying, 'Hello lads,' before adding, 'you're both welcome to come to our house for something to eat, if you want.' Billy and I were a bit dubious, to tell the truth, envisaging quiet country lanes and guns and dead bodies. Finally, we both looked at each other, nodded and said, 'Thanks, yes, we'll go.'

They drove us about five miles out of town to a run-down council estate in the shadow of the hills which surround Belfast. Entering the house we were struck by the sight which greeted us in the living room. There was a woman of about 40 years of age, lying on the couch with just her night-gown on. In an armchair sat a blonde female who looked as if she was still in her teens. 'Mum, can I have some money to buy cigarettes?' she asked the older female. 'Do you think I'm made of money?' replied the woman on the couch. I thought, 'Aye, aye, what have we walked into here?' But as soon as all five of us walked into the living room the mother sat up and the young girl's sulky countenance turned to smiles. 'Mum, these lads are from Liverpool. They've come over to watch the match this afternoon,' explained John, her son. The mother looked us and down and said, 'Come in, I'll make you a cup of tea.'

Half an hour later Billy and I were sitting at the kitchen table eating bacon, eggs, sausages, beans and toast. Neither of us could believe how kind these people were being. 'That was lovely that,' I said as the plate was taken away to be washed. 'No problem, son, did you enjoy your food?' asked the mother, whose name turned out to be Grace. 'Yes, thanks,' Billy replied. Soon after, John and Billy said, 'Come on, we're going to the pub.' So, Billy Hignett and I jumped into their car and the five of us drove a couple of miles to a pool hall in the middle of nowhere. Walking in we were immediately ushered into the bar area where drinks were ordered - I had a lager shandy. Looking around the room, there were about 20 young fellas playing pool. Being Belfast, I wondered what denomination they all were. I soon found out because on the far wall was a huge portrait of King William of Orange. I gulped, nudged my mate Billy and hoped nobody would ask what church we attended back in Liverpool. To our host's credit, they didn't ask what religion we were - thank goodness. If they had done I was fully prepared to lie through my teeth, in order to save myself.

After four lager shandy's it was time to leave for the match. Arriving at Crusaders' small ground, which was situated near to the docks, I quickly bought a programme for 10p and then entered the ground. There were Liverpool supporters all over the ground, though mostly of the Irish kind. In all, there must have been around 150 Scousers in the stadium. With the score standing at 2-0 from the first leg, the game was simply a formality. But the Reds responded to the urgings of their large Irish support by putting on a show of strength which eventually led to five goals entering the Crusaders' net, without reply.

After the game, Billy and I thanked our hosts for their generous hospitality and promised to meet up with them if ever they were in Liverpool. 'Look after yourselves, lads,' they shouted and we turned left ground and began the walk back to our ship. It didn't take long - about 25 minutes but we were glad to be back as the British army, for some reason, were out in force after the game. The sight of khaki coloured jeeps and armoured Land-Rovers driving past slightly unnerved both of us. Apparently, there had been trouble between some of the fans outside the ground. The Liverpool contingent weren't involved. Later on, we found out the fighting was between Catholics and Protestants who had been at the game. Must say, I was glad to be out of it. I didn't mind fighting Geordie's last Saturday but there was no way I was getting involved in any trouble with this Belfast crowd. We made it safely back to the docks and after a two hour wait finally boarded the ship and set sail for the Mersey. As the vessel manoeuvred itself out of it's Belfast berth the sailing home party began. The 150 Liverpool supporters congregated in the ship's lounge and, as the ale began flowing, the singing began. All the old Kop songs were sung and, once again, everybody had a great time. The party continued throughout the night before finally breaking up when our ship docked in Liverpool at 7 o'clock on Wednesday morning. The first thing I did on arriving home was to get myself something to eat before retiring to my bed, which I stayed in for the next 12 hours. After the events of the last few days in Newcastle and Belfast, I certainly needed the rest.

●●●●●●●●●●●●●●

MICHELLE TAYLOR
Crisp packer

Chelsea v Liverpool
Stamford Bridge, December 1995

I'm originally from Aylesbury in Buckinghamshire and have been a season ticket holder at Anfield for a number of seasons. My first ever season ticket was for the centenary stand but this season I've moved to the posters on the wall in my bedroom and every time Liverpool played I would either be listening to the match on radio or watching it on the telly. Kenny Dalglish was my first hero and I would collect pictures, posters, anything in fact, of him. I thought he was the best player Liverpool ever had. At home, all my family are Arsenal supporters and, as a kid, I continually had to defend Liverpool FC's honour because I was brought up to believe that the Gunners were THE team to follow. As time went on my family got used to the idea of my supporting the Reds. I took plenty of stick but with Liverpool being so successful I was in a good position to give it back. As I got older I began to journey to Anfield to watch the team in action. There were times when I had very little money but I always managed to beg, steal or borrow the cash to get to Anfield for the match. It used to cost me a lot to follow the Reds. It was all worth it, of course, and the more I saw of them the more I grew to support them. In February 1996 I decided to move up to Liverpool, simply to be nearer to the team I support and love. I now live in a house in Stockbridge Village, which isn't that far from either Liverpool's training ground at Melwood, nor Anfield. It's certainly a lot closer than Aylesbury is, put it that way. My mum and dad were sad to see me leave but they understand why I wanted to move to Liverpool. I think they understand my passion for Liverpool Football Club a bit more now. I still visit them as much as I can and they still give me stick about football whenever I go down to Buckinghamshire.

I started work in a crisp factory in Skelmersdale recently and working shifts, as I do, gives me ample opportunity of travelling to the training ground to meet the players and watch them train. I usually come down to Melwood around two times a week to get autographs and to talk with the players. If I'm on the late shift I'll grab a couple of hours sleep and then come down to the training ground to see the players before going home to bed for a few hours, before leaving for work again. You see the same faces, day in day out at Melwood. They probably come for the very same reasons I come for. We all love being near to the Liverpool players. Since meeting the players I've found all of them to be a great bunch of lads, though, I must say, Neil Ruddock is my favourite player. I've always liked his style of play and, apart from that, his personality is terrific. He's always laughing and joking and always finds time to chat with the fans who congregate at the training ground. I've spoken to him on a number of occasions and he always has a kind word to say.

I don't go to as many away matches as I would wish but I went to Chelsea last season and found myself being photographed and interviewed by a magazine outside Stamford Bridge.

How it happened was that my friend, Sharon Howe, and myself travelled down to my parents by train a couple of days before the game. We stayed there until Saturday morning and then made our way, again by train, to Stamford Bridge. This was my first visit to Chelsea's ground and it showed because we both got lost on the way. A chap had directed us onto the wrong train from Aylesbury and we ended up miles from anywhere. Luckily, we had plenty of time to redeem the situation and eventually we arrived at Victoria Station, in London, in good time to catch our underground connection to Fulham Broadway. We arrived at the ground around 1pm and we went and bought something to eat before making our way to the ground. Both Sharon and I were dressed in the Liverpool kit and as we were walking around Stamford Bridge we were accosted by a couple who said, 'Excuse me, can we interview you for the Super Liverpool magazine.' They asked who my favourite player was and what was the first match I ever went to? Then they asked if I would mind if they put my answers in the magazine. I said, 'Not at all. I'd be really pleased if you did.' They then took our photographs and thanked us. Sharon and I were really excited at the prospect of appearing in the Super Liverpool magazine. After the interview all the Liverpool supporters around us were asking, 'Hey girl, who were they?' When they found out, the fans tried to get the couple to interview them as well. Both of us were thinking, 'Fame at last,' but when the magazine came out the following month we couldn't see our photographs inside. I got in touch with them and they said there had been a few problems with the negatives and, as a consequence, they hadn't been able to print our photos. Sharon and I were really disappointed at not appearing in the magazine. But at least they used our quotes, which was better than nothing, I suppose.

● ● ● ● ● ● ● ● ● ● ● ● ● ●

IAN BROWN
Lift Engineer

Various games from the 1970's & 1980's

I remember going to watch Liverpool play Nottingham Forest twice in the same season. The first game was that infamous European Cup first round tie which we lost 2-0. The second was the league game which was played in April 1979, near to the end of the season, which finished 0-0. In the league game my mates and I were standing on the terracing at the side of the pitch (that's where the away supporters were put in those days), and there were two blonde girls who said they were Liverpool supporters standing right in front of us. I think they were from Nottingham because they were telling us about certain pubs they normally went to in the town centre. Apparently, they loved the Scouse accent and they kept asking us to say something in 'Scouse.' We got talking to them and one of my mates, a lad called Stevie Boyd, from Old Swan, dived on one of them - then struggled a bit - before coming back up with the girl's bra. He proceeded to tie this bra around his head and then put the cup over his mouth. All through the game he stood there with this bra cup over his mouth. At half-time he changed cups while the girl was pleading with him to give her back her bra. Before the end of the game one of the girls got dragged to the back of the terracing before being waylaid by a number of randy Scousers.

Earlier that season we had gone to Nottingham for the European Cup game against them. They scored after three minutes with a goal from Garry Birtles. Liverpool totally dominated the match after that but near the end they broke away and scored again through Barrett. When he scored the whole Liverpool end of the terracing emptied straight away. The belief was that the Liverpool supporters were so sick at going 2-0 down they had decided to go home early. In reality, they had charged round to the Nottingham end, which was behind the goal, and forced their way onto their terracing. In the subsequent melee the Nottingham Forest fans all ran down to the front to escape the wrath of the Liverpool supporters. Outside the ground it was even worse because scores of Forest fans were literally being thrown into the River Trent. On the bridge the fans were going berserk, throwing home supporters over the parapet and into the water below. Car windows were being put in - bottles and bricks were being thrown by Liverpool supporters, who were sick at getting beaten 2-0. I've seen Liverpool fans rioting before but nothing was ever as bad as that night in Nottingham.

For some reason the Liverpool and Nottingham Forest supporters never really got on that well. I think that had something to do with the style of play that Brian Clough's side employed each time they played Liverpool. They would always play on the break, even at home. They would defend in numbers and then break out of defence to score. We never seemed to have any luck against them. Everything they did always seemed to come off. In my opinion, that's why the Liverpool supporters hated Nottingham Forest to the degree they did.

After the rioting had taken place on the bridge the Liverpool supporters made their way back to the station to catch their special trains home. All the fans piled aboard and the train we were on set off. When we arrived outside Uttoxeter around 11pm somebody pulled the communication cord and suddenly everybody jumped off the train and started walking toward the town centre. My mates and I stayed on the train, because we were getting a bit old in the tooth for all that lark, by minutes later all the fans climbed back on board carrying jewellery, clothes, watches, carpets, three piece suites. We walked down the train later on and it was like Paddy's market on a Saturday morning. Everybody was bartering the gear they had robbed. Lads were parading around saying, 'Anybody wanna buy a Rolex?......only a fiver!' I'm sure if you had needed a gas fire somebody would have been able to come up with the goods that night.

When the train was pulling into Edge Hill the communication cord got pulled again and about 400 lads jumped off and ran across the tracks. They knew full well that the police would be waiting for them when the train eventually pulled into Lime Street. When we did arrive at the station there were hundreds of police waiting for us, but by this time, there were only about 40 supporters left on the train, and all of them were 'clean.'

* * * *

From 1975 to 1981 I used to follow Liverpool everywhere - and I mean everywhere! Even to the likes of Southend for a midweek League Cup tie. Come to think of it, I must have been fucking mad. We used to travel to most away games by car. My mate, Ian Lowe, used to have this Ford Capri, which was his pride and joy, and he would drive us to these away games. The thing with Lowey, though, was that he was a terrible loser. He couldn't stand it when Liverpool got beat. We'd been to watch Liverpool at Maine Road one Easter - Liverpool had won 4-0, by the way. We were stuck in traffic outside the ground and a Manchester City fan, having spied Lowey's Liverpool FC sticker on the back window, decided to spit on his windscreen, as he walked past. Lowey looked at the big yokker on the window, and then he looked at the fella. Next thing, he turned the engine off, picked up his Krooklok, got out of the car, shouted the lad, who turned round, and then he hit him over the head with the Krooklok. The lad went down while the Krooklok bent under the   force of the blow. There were loads of people around so, in order to save him from being arrested, we were shouting, 'Lowey, get in the fucking car, will yer!' He just stood over the fella and said, 'No one fucking gobs on me motor!' The lad was out of the game by this time, but Lowey never relented, screaming, 'Now look what you've done, you've broke me fucking Krooklok, yer bastard!'

Don't get me wrong, Lowey was a nice fella but if anybody got the wrong side of him he'd fucking batter them. Old Trafford is another example of what I'm talking about. We'd gone there for a league game and had parked the car on Warwick Road. Four of us were walking down toward the Scoreboard End. Two of us had walked on ahead, thinking we would be safer walking apart from each other (you know what Old Trafford is like!). Next thing, we heard a commotion behind us and there's Lowey, who's got this scarf seller up against the wall with a scarf round his neck, trying to strangle him. He's shouting, 'Yer Manc bastard!' Apparently, the scarf seller had been selling 'Shankly '81' scarves and Lowey had took offence at this. All the local lads knew he was a Scouser by now but none of them dared approach him. Knowing Lowey as I do, I couldn't blame them because he was a scary guy. He was about 6ft 3ins and about 18 stone and could handle himself. When he got angry there was something about his eyes which told you not to go near him. We said to him later, 'We thought we were going to keep out of trouble, today?' Lowey said, 'I know, but I just lost it when I saw that scarf.'

* * * *

My own brother, Stan was another fella who you wouldn't care to mess with. I remember sitting behind the goal at Maine Road one day reading the programme before the game. I heard a disturbance coming from the Kippax and looking across you could see a big circle which had opened up in the middle of the terracing. In the middle of this circle were four or five lads fighting with fellas who were congregating on the outer rim of the circle. My mate Jimmy said, 'I'm sure that's you're Stan fighting there.' My brother used to have really blonde hair and all I could see was this blonde head scrapping with the Manchester City fans. In the middle of this circle with him were members of his gang, who were from Childwall. They were, Gabby, Howey, Satch, Bonehead, Bernie and Jugger. All seven of them had decided to take the Kippax, that day. I'll tell you, they had a good go as well.

You had to know our Stan because, around that time - from 1975 to 1981, there was nobody to touch him - he was a complete and utter nutter - and I mean that! There was nothing he wouldn't do. Him and his gang from Childwall had no fear, whatsoever. They used to try things that nobody else would do, like taking on armies of home supporters at away grounds. They wouldn't bother going into the Liverpool end. They would invariably try and enter the home end of the ground - just to fight with their boys. But back to this Manchester City game. Our Stan was fighting with their supporters but I wasn't scared for him because I knew the type of people he was with. He eventually got marched out of the Kippax by three policemen. They had his arm right up his back but as he passed behind the goal he must have seen us because he waved and shouted, 'Ian, I'll see you later!' The police suddenly started pointing toward us and gesturing to their colleagues who were standing nearer to where we were sitting. They obviously thought we were part of the same gang. In the end, we had to leave the ground because otherwise we would have gotten arrested - no doubts! Because of our Stan, we missed the game. We ran back in at three-quarter time but because he'd waved at us we'd missed the game.

PAUL EATON
Football Journalist

Spartak Moscow v Liverpool
European Cup Winners Cup tie,
October 1992

If I sat down and analysed my reasons for going to see Liverpool play Spartak Moscow in Russia I probably wouldn't be able to tell you. Thinking back, I must have been mad because I didn't even have the money to pay for the trip in the first place. I actually went into terrible debt to get myself over to Russia. Whatsmore, I wasn't even earning any wages at that time as I was a full time journalism student at college. I couldn't even claim any dole money; so why on earth I decided to travel all the way to Russia is still a mystery to me four years hence. But the important thing, as a committed Liverpool fan, was that I was there. And, that last statement probably explains the reasons why. My friend, Lee Miller, had just celebrated his birthday with the result that he had come into money. He was desperate to go to the game but he didn't want to go by himself, which was understandable. He suggested that I borrow the required amount from him and that's why I was able to go.

Lee and I had originally booked a two day/one night trip with Duggan Holidays, who have since gone bust - but that's another story! The trip would have cost us £250- which wasn't bad. But, almost at the last minute, the travel company informed us they had decided to cancel their planned excursion - 'Because of a general lack of interest.' I didn't believe a word of it. We only found out they had cancelled the trip after I had telephoned their offices to check our departure and arrival times. When I did they haughtily informed me that the plane had been cancelled. I said, 'What, well why didn't you tell us earlier.' The girl on the other end of the line said, 'We were going to inform all the fans by letter.' Seeing as

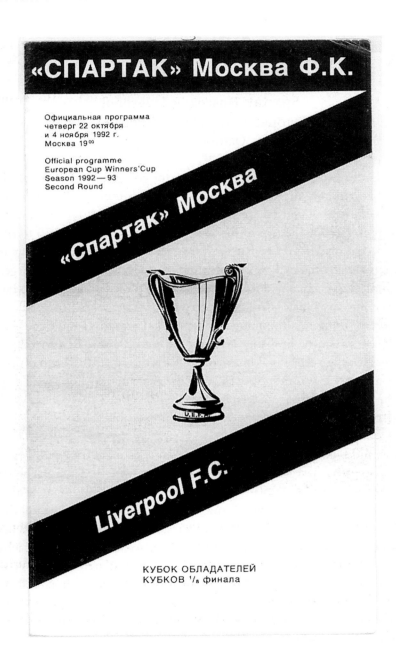

it was only two days before departure I thought they were leaving things a bit late. To cut a long story short, Lee and I then managed to book a trip costing £450 with another travel company. On a personal level, my debt to Lee was now mounting up in alarming fashion. We finally confirmed our bookings the day before we were due to leave and as excitement mounted at the thought of travelling to a foreign country I began to pack my bags.

We left Manchester Airport for the four and a half hour flight to Moscow on Monday, two days before the game was due to be played. There were around 50 Liverpool supporters on the plane and the journey to Russia was pretty uneventful with the fans laughing and singing as the miles flew by. We eventually landed in Moscow and as soon as our feet hit the tarmac we were all struck by the intensity of the cold weather - it was freezing! Luckily, we didn't have to wait around for too long because a bus came to pick us up to take the fans to the hotel we'd been booked into. The hotel itself, which was called the Salut Hotel, situated in the centre of Moscow, wasn't exactly a five star establishment. To be brutally honest, it was a hovel. Apparently, it was supposed to be one of the best hotels in the city. If that was the case, I wouldn't have liked to have stayed in the worst. Lee decided to have a shower on the first night and that was the only shower he did take because he found himself sharing the bathroom with a huge cockroach. The insect wouldn't vacate the premises so Lee decided he would instead. The food they served us was literally inedible. We had chicken and chips on the first night but the chips were literally black. I don't know what kind of oil they cooked them in but it sure wasn't like the stuff at home. We refused to eat ours and instead went looking for something to eat around Moscow. Macdonalds had opened their first ever restaurant in Russia the year before and, as fate would have it, the place was just around the corner from where we were staying. Lee and I hightailed over to there and spent the next hour or so eating good old American food. I ordered two Big Macs, an apple pie and a coke, which, would you believe, came to only 20p in our money. We couldn't believe it and so after polishing off the Big Macs we went and ordered two more, just to be sociable, you understand.

We got back to the hotel and spent an uncomfortable night trying to sleep on rock hard beds which must have been about 100 years old. Outside, the wind howled and the snow fell in huge flakes. It must have been around -10 degrees outside. It wasn't much warmer inside because the heating wasn't working and the blankets we had weren't enough to fully keep out the cold. It was at this point I wondered if I'd done the right thing in coming to watch Liverpool play in Russia. The next morning most of the Liverpool supporters, having heard about Macdonalds, were to be found eating their breakfast in there. The manager of the hotel must have wondered where his guests had disappeared to but knowing what the hotel food was like it was no surprise to see the breakfast tables empty. In the afternoon the Liverpool

Кубок обладателей кубков
1/8 финала
четверг 22 октября 1992 г. 19⁰⁰

«Спартак» Москва   Ливерпуль Ф.К.

Ч. Черчесов   Д. Джеймс
Д. Хлестов   Р. Джонс
А. Иванов   Д. Барроуз
Д. Попов   Я. Мольбю
М. Русяев   Р. Уиллан
А. Чернышов   М. Райт
В. Онопко   С. Макмэнаман
В. Карпин   П. Стюарт
А. Пятницкий   Я. Раш
И. Ледяхов   М. Уолтерс
Д. Радченко   М. Томас

Г. Стауче   Б. Гроббелар
Р. Мамедов   М. Марш
О. Кужлев   Н. Таннер
В. Бесчастных   Р. Розенталь
Н. Писарев   Ж. Редкнапп
А. Татаркин   М. Хуппер

О. Романцев   Г. Сунесс

                Судья в поле —
                Судьи на линиях —

Attention F. C. «Liverpool» supporters
Dear friends, F. C. «Spartak» Moscow
propose you to exchange the souvenirs
(badges, scarft, programmes) of all
Russian clubs on the souvenirs of British
clubs
Our adress: 125195 Moscow Russia
              Troubetskoj   Wjacheslav
              /до востребования/

Программа отпечатана в поли-
графической фирме «Кр. пр.».
Тир. 2000 экз. Заказ № 6101.

tour of Moscow. There were some remarkable sights, including scores of beggars who, on finding we were from the west, were literally on their hands and knees begging for money. One fella even offered to sell me his dog. I didn't buy it but I gave him a few rubles, so he could buy himself some food. There was snow and ice on the ground and it was absolutely freezing but, apparently, these people live on the streets all the time. I don't know how they cope. We ended up in Kremlin Square and saw Liverpool secretary, Peter Robinson, along with Mark Lawrenson, giving tickets out to one or two individuals. One of the Liverpool supporters shouted, 'Aye, aye, Peter, doing a bit of touting, are you?' Peter Robinson gave the guy a disdainful look and then merely walked away. I thought aloud, 'He could have been a bit more cheerful, there!'

In the evening, Lee and I decided we would go and watch a football match being played in the same stadium which Liverpool were playing at the following night. With the cost of living being so low we decided to travel to the game in style by ordering a taxi. Not many Russians travel by this mode of transport and, as a result, there is never much work for taxi drivers. We learnt this during the journey to the stadium as our driver explained, in broken English, that he would wait for us outside the ground until after the game. We weren't bothered about the clock being on either because the cost of the taxi was so inexpensive - pennies, in fact. The match was a European tie between CSKA Moscow and Barcelona. There were only about 30,000 fans watching the game in a stadium which could have held 100,000. We paid our money to get in (I can't remember how much it cost, but it was very cheap) and sat down behind one of the goals, to view the game. It was so cold that five minutes into the game both of us were praying for the final whistle. I know the weather can get bad in this country but it could never have been as cold as it was inside the Lenin Stadium that night. By half-time we'd had enough and decided to head back to the relative warmth of our hotel. We'd been warned by our travel agent not to travel alone at any time but we hadn't heeded the warning fully. As a result, I was almost mugged in the toilet inside our hotel. A Russian guy sidled up to me and, spotting my expensive camera, began pulling on it. I managed to resist his determined efforts and ran back into the safety of the hotel foyer, where most of the Liverpool supporters were situated.

Come mid-afternoon on the day of the game and we began getting ready for the match itself. Our coach arrived about two hours before the game was due to kick-off and the 50 Liverpool supporters got on board. The journey to the stadium took about 30 minutes and after we had disembarked outside the ground we immediately showed our tickets to the gateman. This first set of gates was a good quarter of a mile from the main turnstiles, and we had to walk the remaining distance, just to gain entrance into the ground itself. Having attended the previous night's game between CSKA Sofia and Barcelona, Lee and I were struck by the difference in crowd size. There were at least double the amount of fans inside the stadium - at least 60,000 - 70,000. The atmosphere was terrific, too, considering most of the stadium was open to the elements. But, as in the previous night, it was still horribly cold. So cold that you couldn't hardly breathe, at times. I hadn't realised this before setting off from England and, as a consequence, had to try and keep warm wearing only a Liverpool top and leather jacket.

As you know, Liverpool went down by four goals to two, with Steve McManaman and Mark Wright getting the goals for us. When Bruce Grobelaar got sent off we feared the worst - and the worst was to come. David Burrows went in goal for the remainder of the game and his heroics couldn't save us from an ignominious defeat. Coming out of the ground after the game, the Liverpool fans I spoke to knew that we would have a struggle on our hands in the second leg at Anfield, a fortnight hence.

We stayed in Moscow that night and for most of the next day, which included another sight-seeing tour. By this stage, all I wanted to do was to go home. I was relieved and happy when the time for departure finally arrived. We landed in Manchester Airport on Friday morning and drove back to Liverpool as soon as customs were cleared. On reflection, I'm glad I went on the trip but, I don't think I would ever go to Russia again......not unless Lee offered to lend me the money, again!

● ● ● ● ● ● ● ● ● ● ● ● ● ●

JOHN GARNER
Plumber

Auxerre v Liverpool
UEFA Cup tie

A group of us from Halewood decided to forsake the comfort and pleasures of the organised trips which the club had laid on, for the excitement and adventure of a cross-country jaunt through France by train. We booked our tickets on the older person's equivalent of Transalpino. I can't remember how much the tickets cost but it wasn't that expensive. We'd looked at the possibilities of travelling by coach but didn't fancy driving all the way to Auxerre, arriving an hour before the game kicked off, and then being shepherded back onto the coach for the return journey. That sort of trip is alright if you're a kid but not when you fancy doing a bit of sightseeing, which is what we did.

The first leg of our journey took us from Lime Street to Euston station, in London. From there we travelled by underground to Waterloo and then caught the ferry train to Dover. We landed in Calais before catching our connection to Paris. We stayed in Paris for the day and then jumped on a train to Auxerre, which is down toward the southern part of France. When we eventually arrived in the town itself we were duly impressed by the medieval flavour of the place. It reminded me very much of Chester, with old style buildings set amid an impressive backdrop of snow covered mountains in the distance. There were plenty of Liverpudlians who had made the trip but the vast majority of them didn't arrive until just a few hours before the game. Having travelled under our own steam we had the place, more or less, to ourselves. We had a few drinks in the bars around the town centre and swapped souvenirs and memorabilia with the home supporters. The Auxerre fans were really friendly toward us and we were getting our photographs taken with a lot of them. The afternoon wore on and, having secured our tickets for the game, we finally entered the stadium. The Liverpool supporters, having arrived in the town an hour or so earlier, began to let off steam inside the ground. They were making a lot of noise before the game. When the two teams arrived on the pitch the Liverpudlians really began cheering their team on. Unfortunately, on the night, it wasn't enough because Auxerre scored two goals, without reply. Funnily enough, I was still confident that Liverpool could overturn the deficit in the second leg, at Anfield.

After travelling all that way our group decided after the match that we didn't fancy catching the train back to Calais. This would have involved waiting for hours at various stations for different connections. Instead, we split up and managed to cadge a lift back to the French port from some Liverpool supporters. We arrived in Calais a good few hours before we were due to and, as a consequence, were able to catch an earlier ferry back to England. We arrived back in Liverpool sometime on Thursday afternoon, which was great, considering the distance we'd had to travel.

Before I finish describing the tie against Auxerre I must mention the second leg because it is still vivid in my memory. As I said before, I always fancied Liverpool to beat the French team on home soil. For the preceding two weeks leading up to the second leg, confidence seemed to grow amongst Liverpudlians that the team could actually overcome the two goal deficit. On the day of the game all the newspapers had, more or less, written us off. I loved it when they did that because it gave the supporters, not to mention the team, something to prove. There were only twenty odd thousand fans inside Anfield that night, but what a night it proved to be. I think the supporters who did turn up were the real hard-core Liverpool supporters - and they were mostly Scousers! I sensed something special could happen as soon as I walked into the ground. I don't know, I just felt an atmosphere as the Liverpool team warmed up before the game. Apparently, the Auxerre players, while doing their warm-ups, were looking around at the empty spaces inside the ground and thinking it was going to be easy. They had heard about the epic European nights at Anfield, in particular, the famous encounter with their fellow countrymen of St. Etienne back in 1977, when the Kop had thundered Liverpool toward the European Cup semi-final with their fanatical and noisy support. They couldn't have realised, looking at the empty seats inside Anfield, that tonight they were in for a surprise of their life. The Kop took the initiative from the kick-off as they urged Liverpool on. We were standing next to a fella who had one of those flares and the sight of those really set the Kop alight. If you were an outsider looking in the whole terracing must have looked like something out of Dante's Inferno. You know what it's like when the Kop are in full voice - it can bring a lump to your throat, especially when you are an opposition player! I wondered what the Auxerre players were thinking as the Kop began to roar Liverpool on. It wasn't just the Kop who were in good vocal form that night because the Kemlyn Road, taking their cue from us, began to sing, which was surprising as you usually rarely hear them. Even the Liverpudlians in the paddock and main stand were singing and chanting. The fans in the Anfield Road end joined in too and very soon their vocal efforts were rewarded when Liverpool pulled back the two goal deficit with goals by Molby and Marsh, the first a penalty. I've rarely heard a noise like it inside Anfield. And to think, there were only twenty odd thousand fans inside the ground. Just imagine the noise we might have made if it had been a full house. When Mark Walters scored the winner there was pandemonium inside Anfield. Just before the third goal went in you could see the French players visibly wilting under the pressure the crowd were putting them under. As shot after shot rained in on the Auxerre goal the noise, which had been at fever pitch already, actually increased. You got the feeling the visiting team had never experienced an atmosphere like it.

When the final whistle blew you could see the French team literally falling down with the sheer exhaustion of the moment. They had been well and truly beaten; not just by the Liverpool team but by the Liverpool supporters, too. I actually felt sorry for fellas who hadn't been to the game, because they certainly missed one of the all-time classic Anfield European ties. People still talk about that Auxerre game. In its own little way, I think it ranks up there with the Inter Milan, Bruges and St. Etienne games, from the 60's and 70's.

If that game was one of the highlights of watching Liverpool I've got to say my own personal highlight was when I scored the last goal in front of the Kop before it got knocked down. If you've got a moment I'll tell you how I managed to achieve this rare feat. It was the final game against Norwich City and, as you know, everybody turned up ready for a party that day. In that respect, I feel the players themselves let us down badly, both in the game itself and afterwards. I know they came out to unfurl that big banner but really I thought they should have stayed with the supporters for longer than they did. It was the last day of the Kop, don't forget, and the players should have realised how much that meant to the Liverpool supporters.

A lot of the supporters had come in fancy dress, me included. To be honest, all our gang from Halewood had agreed beforehand to get dressed up in wacky clothes. But, come the day of the game I found I was the only one who had made a real effort. Don't get me wrong, all my mates had the full red and white gear on but I'd gone a stage further by dressing in a pair of khaki shorts and top, steel toe capped boots and a Tommy Cooper fez on my head. I also had one of those stick-on mous taches. I must have looked a sight, but who cared, it was the last day of the Kop and I was determined to see it off in style.

When the players finally went into the dressing rooms there were still thousands of supporters still left on the Kop. Nobody wanted to leave, as you know. There was a ball lying in the netting in the goal and one of the stewards picked it up and threw it into the Kop. A kid caught hold of it and I said, 'Give us that ball, will you kid?' He gave it to me and I turned to my mate Mono and said, 'I'm getting onto the pitch, are you coming?' He was having none of it and so, when the coppers' backs were turned, I ran up the slope and onto the grass. As soon as the Kop spotted my antics they were roaring their encouragement. The police didn't bother trying to chase me - I think they were rather enjoying the moment themselves. I ran to the edge of the penalty area and then turned to face the Kop. I did a bit of a dribble and headed for goal. The Liverpool supporters were cheering me on as I converged on the goal with this ball at my feet. When I reached the penalty spot I elected to shoot and when the ball hit the back of the net the roar from the Kop reached decibel proportions. I felt great, having scored a goal in front of the famous terracing. I calmly walked back toward my spec but then two policemen grabbed my arm and marched me the length of the pitch toward the Anfield Road end. The Kop were booing the police as they escorted me from the penalty area. As we were walking down the two policemen were asking if I was a season ticket holder. I was but denied being so because they were saying things like, 'You won't get into Anfield ever again for that.' I thought their attitude was a bit over the top. I know they wanted to charge me but when we reached the cells at the Anfield Road end of the ground they asked their sergeant, 'What shall we do with this fella, sarge?' He looked me up and down and replied, 'Just throw him out!' You could tell the two policemen who had grabbed me were really pig-sick at having to let me go. As I walked away, smiling, I said to them, 'And you have a nice day, too!'

After my little jaunt the rest of the Liverpool supporters sensed that was the last of the excitement and they began to make their way out of the Spion Kop for the very last time. I met up with my mates in Sam Dodds afterwards and, after a couple of bevvies, Mono asked me, 'You realise what you've done, don't you?' I said, 'No, what?' He said, 'You've only gone and scored the last goal in front of the Kop.' Realising this, I was chuffed to bits. That wasn't the end of the matter because within days the Liverpool Echo got in touch asking if they could do an article on me. A photographer came and took my photo and they did a story on me, which was featured prominently in the inside back page of the paper. A couple of weeks later I decided to take the whole thing a stage further by spraying the steel toe capped boot, the one I'd scored with, in gold. We had been planning a charity night in aid of the Roy Castle appeal in the Leather Bottle pub in Halewood and, to coincide with this function, I donated my golden boot to help boost funds. On the night the place was packed to the rafters and everybody congratulated me on being the last ever person to score a goal in front of the famous Spion Kop. It was a truly proud moment for me and one I'll never forget.

● ● ● ● ● ● ● ● ● ● ● ● ●

TERRY COTEY
Student Teacher

Barnsley v Liverpool
FA Cup quarter final, March 1985

Barnsley were a second division side when they were drawn to play Liverpool in the sixth round of that season's FA Cup. The previous week Leeds United's fans had wreaked havoc at Oakwell when they threw missiles at the disabled enclosure, inside the ground. There had been further trouble outside the ground after the game between warring supporters on both sides. As a consequence, Liverpool's hooligan element

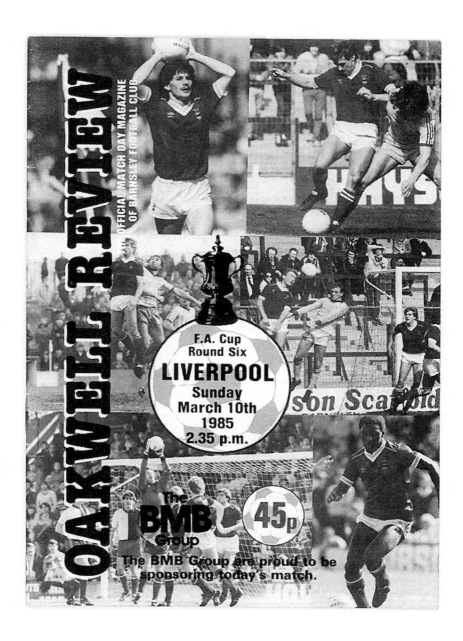

up for this Sunday afternoon encounter. Plenty of supporters made the trip to Yorkshire for the cup tie, either by car, coach or train. My friends and I chose the latter option because we wanted to be in Barnsley town centre in good time for the game. There were about 150 lads on board our train, which departed around 10.30 on Sunday morning. Nobody knew what to expect because none of us had ever been to Barnsley's ground before. As our train reached the outskirts of the town you could tell we were in mining country, with slag heaps and collieries dotted around the countryside. Viewing the surroundings, the Liverpool supporters were taking the piss, shouting, 'fucking woolybacks,' out of the windows as the train passed through various suburban stations.

We arrived at Barnsley around 12.30 and as soon as we had exited the station the supporters from the train began the 20 minute walk to the ground. Being a Sunday there were hardly any shops open but when we did find a shop we all piled in and got something to eat and drink. Some fans didn't pay for what they had taken, but that's nothing out of the ordinary, I suppose. After we'd come out of there we had another 10 minute walk to the ground. As we approached the stadium, which was in a valley, we began to realise that maybe today wouldn't be such a walkover, as many of the Liverpool lads had presumed. There were mobs of Barnsley boys standing on each corner, carefully scrutinising our mob. Nobody came near us but you got the feeling they were weighing up the options before making their move later that afternoon.

When we got into the ground we saw their boys on the opposite terrace, taunting the travelling Liverpool army with songs and chants. The most impressive, I suppose, was that familiar refrain, 'You Scouse bastards,' repeated ad infinitum. We replied with a chant of our own: 'Sheep-shaggers, nah, nah, nah,' etc. That shut them up for a couple of minutes before they launched into that classic terrace warning, 'You're gonna get you're fucking heads kicked in.' It was pre-match entertainment at its best. When the match kicked off Barnsley strove to create an early

Team Line-ups

BARNSLEY
Shirts: Red
Shorts: White
Stockings: Red

1 Clive BAKER
2 Joe JOYCE
3 Nicky LAW
4 Billy RONSON
5 Larry MAY
6 Paul FUTCHER
7 Gordon OWEN
8 Gwyn THOMAS
9 Ron FUTCHER
10 Steve AGNEW
11 Winston CAMPBELL
12

LIVERPOOL
Shirts: Yellow
Shorts: Yellow
Stockings: Yellow

1 Bruce GROBBELAAR
2 Phil NEAL
3 Alan KENNEDY
4 Mark LAWRENSON
5 Steve NICHOLS
6 Alan HANSEN
7 Kenny DALGLISH
8 Ronnie WHELAN
9 Ian RUSH
10 Kevin MacDONALD
11 John WARK
12

Referee: C. Downey, Harlow, Middlesex.
Red Flag: T.F. Hill, Lincoln.
Yellow Flag: G. Banwell, Stafford.

The Man in the Middle

COLIN DOWNEY (Harlow, Middlesex).

A systems analyst in the computer business, Colin Downey is married, with one son. He started refereeing in 1965 and progressed via the Spartan and Isthmian Leagues. He is interested in cricket, squash and badminton and is chairman of the Hounslow R.A. He regularly officiates in National and London five-a-sides; refereed in the Atari '6' tournament in 1983, and was senior linesman in the F.A. Cup Final the same year.

didn't come. At half-time the score stood at 0-0. In the second period Liverpool gained the ascendancy and within ten minutes of the restart took the lead with a goal from Ian Rush. Ronnie Whelan scored a second before Rushie replied with two late goals which saw us into the semi-finals of the FA Cup. Coming out of the ground there was a feeling that something was about to kick-off - and I'm not talking about football. Liverpool's mob was quite large, by this stage. In terms of numbers, there must have been about 800 of us who walked back toward the town centre. As we came to within half a mile of the railway station we heard a great roar coming from a side street. I was near the back of our mob and suddenly I saw around 300 Barnsley boys attacking the Liverpool fans at the front. Suddenly, all hell let loose as the Liverpool supporters began fighting back. 'Come on, Scousers, don't run,' somebody up ahead shouted. Next thing, we chased the Barnsley boys down the side street they had just come from. We chased them for about 200 yards before they turned and charged at us. It was quite scary, at this stage, because a lot of them were big miners, who had joined in the fray. We were just lads, but we had the advantage in terms of numbers. 'Get them,' one of the Barnsley ring-leaders shouted, and around 50 of their mob broke away and tried to outflank the Liverpool mob. Fists and boots flew as the two armies joined battle in this side street. A roar went up as more of Liverpool's mob piled in from the main road. Bricks and bottles were being thrown. One of my mates had a can of coke which he'd just bought and he decided to throw it into their mob. He couldn't miss because they were just a sea of heads, which were ten or 20 deep. Eventually, through force of numbers, Liverpool's mob gained the upper hand. When the fighting had died down the main body of Liverpool supporters made their way back to the station. When we reached our train, which was standing on the platform, we were suddenly bombarded with bricks and bottles from the other side of a 20 foot wall which lay between us and the Barnsley supporters. A few Liverpool fans got hit by flying glass and one lad took a terrible bashing when a half-brick hit him on the head. We wanted to run out of the station to confront the enemy but were police presence. We got on the train and, as it left the station, we had to duck for our lives as more bricks and bottles crashed into the windows of our carriage. The onslaught continued for the time it took the train to leave the confines of the railway sidings we were in. Five minutes later, with everybody on the train either, bashed, battered or buzzing with the excitement of the fight, the inquests began. The general consensus of opinion, biased though it was, was that our mob had gained a famous victory. No doubt, Barnsley's mob would arrive at a different verdict when they held their own inquest. But at least talking about the day's fighting helped alleviate the boredom of the train journey home.

● ● ● ● ● ● ● ● ● ● ● ● ●

JOHN GARNER
Plumber

Genoa v Liverpool
UEFA Cup tie

The Italian police tried to make the whole trip a military operation because as soon as we landed at Genoa Airport they stood guard over the 100 or so Liverpool supporters who had come by plane. They had arranged buses to take us to, what was literally, a service station, situated a few miles outside the city. The lads I was with, who were mostly from Halewood, didn't fancy being cooped up all day in a poxy service station and so we made plans to escape the escort as soon as the plane had taxied to a halt on the runway. As the vast majority of Liverpool fans began boarding the waiting single decker buses, a group of around five of us did our impression of the Great Escape. We legged it toward the perimeter fence, which was about a quarter of a mile away. Luckily, the Italian police didn't see us at first and so we had a head-start on them. We reached the fence, which was about ten foot high and managed to scale it without any problems. Once outside the airport perimeter we ran as far as the main street and then relaxed, knowing we'd be able to enjoy ourselves for the rest of the day, without any hassle from the Italian police.

We spent the next few hours, indeed the rest of the day, enjoying ourselves. We visited various bars in the city centre and spread the gospel according to Liverpool FC. There were Genoa supporters everywhere but, in the main, they were very friendly. One or two Scousers were up to their usual tricks in the shopping arcades but, apart from that, the day was pretty quiet. As late afternoon turned to evening we began to make our way on foot to the ground. It was then we saw a bit of trouble between rival Genoa and Liverpool supporters, but really it was a storm in a tea-cup. The Italian fans were baiting the Liverpudlians with chants and gestures. The Liverpool fans retaliated by chasing the Genoan supporters down a sidestreet. There were very few blows thrown and after a couple of minutes everything returned to normal. Once inside the ground I was immensely impressed with the layout of the ground. They had, what looked like, turrets on each corner of the stadium. The atmosphere inside was electric - and I mean, electric. I've been to many matches involving Liverpool but rarely have I experienced an atmosphere like the one in Genoa that night. The home supporters really gave it their all. The main body of their support lay at the side of the pitch - the side which housed that huge flag. That's where their main singing mob were situated. But, to tell the truth, all four sides of the ground were filled with singing, chanting Genoa supporters. They had given us the bottom part of the terracing, to the right of the main stand. Unfortunately, in terms of acoustics, this part of the ground was open, which meant our singing wasn't as amplified as the rest of the ground. We tried hard to make a noise but it was virtually impossible to make ourselves heard above the din which the Italian supporters made, both before and during the game.

The game itself didn't go Liverpool's way at all. We enjoyed one or two chances, but, in the main, Genoa always looked like the more likely side to score. As you know, they did - twice! When it was 1-0 we thought there was still a chance of making up the deficit in the return leg at Anfield. But once that second goal went in, from a free kick just outside the box, we knew there was very little chance of overcoming them. We came out of the ground bitterly disappointed and slowly made our way back to the buses which took us back to the airport. There was a bit of trouble a few hundred yards from the stadium when a group of around 50 skinhead scooter boys accosted our mob. It was no contest because the Liverpool fans just charged them. The Italians, on seeing the Scouser's aggressive intent, sped off at high speed, moments before the mob finally caught up with them. We arrived home in Speke a few hours later and everybody agreed it had been a good trip. It was just a pity about the final score, which ultimately led to our exit from that season's competition.

● ● ● ● ● ● ● ● ● ● ● ● ●

GARY OYITCH
Postman

Various Liverpool reserve away games

I originally hail from Boston in Lincolnshire, and I began taking an avid interest in the Reds after watching the 1977 European Cup final between Liverpool and Borussia Moenchen Gladbach in Rome. I was nine years of age at the time and I remember watching the game on telly. I was so pleased at Liverpool winning the European Cup that I became a Reds supporter from that moment on. I used to play for the school football team and we played in red, so I figure that had a bearing on my future footballing allegiances. A group of us would travel from Boston to every 'home' game in a hired car. It cost a lot but I always looked upon it money well spent. The first game I went to at Anfield was against Oxford United in the 1987/88 season. Liverpool beat them 2-0 that day. I was captivated by the Kop. In fact, I was standing outside the ground before the game and got talking to a lad who told me the only place to be was in the middle of the Kop. I took his advice and, despite the pushing and shoving, which I soon got used to, I really enjoyed being part of the Liverpool crowd. Of course, I'd seen Anfield on telly but nothing compared to the real thing. It was tremendous to be a part of the singing and chanting which went on that day. I was buzzing for weeks afterwards, I can tell you!

Living in Lincolnshire, as I did, it was always a long haul getting to Anfield for first team games and so, three years ago, I made a decision to move up to Liverpool. I was working as a fork-lift truck driver in a printers in Boston and when the chance of voluntary redundancy came I took it and relocated to Liverpool. There was another reason for moving and that was my girlfriend, who has since become my wife. I'd met her at a party on the Wirral which some football friends of mine had thrown. I'd only met them through going to the games and, as fate would have it, found my future wife at this party. She is a Liverpool supporter too and so we decided I would move to Liverpool to be next to the great love of my life - Liverpool Football Club. Only joking, love! Living so close to Anfield I began enjoying the luxury of having a lie-in on a Saturday morning because, in contrast, when I lived in Boston, I used to have to get out of bed at 5am and then undertake a five hour journey to Liverpool to see the match. It's great now because I can literally leave my house in Garston at around 1.30pm and be at Anfield by car in less than 25 minutes - and that's with traffic hold-ups, too!

I've always taken a keen interest in every Liverpool team. By that I mean the reserves as well as the A and B teams. I enjoy watching these games because it gives you the opportunity of seeing the young lads progressing through the ranks. Watching the first team is brilliant, of course, but I also get great pleasure from watching the other Liverpool teams in action. In fact, there have even been two occasions when I've actually missed a first team game in order to watch the minor Reds' side in action. This was when Liverpool played Burnley twice in the 1994/95 season. I went to Southport to watch Liverpool play in a Senior Cup tie, instead. The main reason I decided to forsake the first team that night was because I desperately wanted the programme from the Liverpool Senior Cup tie. I'm an avid collector of programmes, team sheets and other memorabilia connected with Liverpool Football Club. At the last count, I had roughly 3,600 Liverpool programmes in my collection. That includes first team, reserves and youth team programmes. There is actually a burgeoning market for this sort of memorabilia, which also includes single team sheets which most clubs produce for the reserve team fixtures. You very rarely get a 'proper' programme being published for these type of games. The fans who attend the reserve matches have to make do with a single sheet with the letterhead printed in the colours of the club concerned and two single columns detailing the teams and substitutes for the game in question. As I say, you very rarely get anything more substantial than that. But, saying that, these team sheets do fetch a reasonable price on the market. Fans advertise in magazines like Programme Monthly and Boot, which are two specialist publications which cater solely for people like myself who collect this type of memorabilia.

Travelling to the away reserve games like I do you get to know the players and coaching staff. They also get used to seeing you at these games and sometimes they will acknowledge your presence by waving as they come out of the tunnel. The reserve team coach, Sammy Lee, gives us complimentary tickets now and again and little things like that do make it all seem worthwhile, especially when you might have travelled 80 miles after a hard days work to watch them play. I've been to all sorts of places with the reserves; places like Barrow, Morecambe, Gateshead, Bridlington, which is where Liverpool have played pre-season friendly games in previous seasons. Mind you, it's so difficult to get the information on the reserve team are playing sometimes. Getting hold of a pre-season fixture list is like trying to find gold dust. It's well nigh impossible. When you telephone the club they will say, 'Oh, you will have to get in touch with Melwood.' When you do telephone the training ground the person on the other end of the line invariably asks in an accusing manner, 'How did you get this telephone number?' before brushing you're request off with a polite but firm, 'Sorry, I can't really give that information out!' I really can't understand why they won't give the information out because it's not as if we're about to rampage and pillage these towns which Liverpool reserves are playing in.

They're are a group of around five or six Liverpool supporters who travel to most of the reserve away games. We all treat it as a night out - with our cups of Bovril and beef crisps at the ready - we really go to town at these away games! It's also enjoyable visiting all these strange grounds, which play host to Liverpool, sometimes. The likes of Barrow and Morecambe, the latter of which, incidentally, is the only club which produces a proper programme for the reserves and youth team games.

Liverpool's decision to play their reserve team games at Southport's Haig Avenue ground was something which our mob were unreservedly against. To be honest, it wasn't so bad at the beginning because we treated it as a novelty. But as time went on it became a bit of a grind, having to endure a 60 mile round trip for each 'home' game. In the end, a group of us wrote to Peter Robinson, Liverpool FC's chief executive, asking if it would be possible to move back to Anfield. We didn't even get a reply back from him. We didn't really enjoy going to Southport to watch Liverpool reserves because we got the impression that the Southport people actually resented us being there. We always struggled to pick up a programme and if any were available they always made it hard for you to get your hands on one of them. I think Liverpool reserves played 26 times at Haig Avenue, and, despite the lack of welcome, I only missed two of those games. The reason for my absence from those fixtures was my wife, Sarah, was giving birth to our son, Matthew.

One reserve game which sticks in my mind was the Nottingham Forest v Liverpool game at the City Ground, a couple of seasons ago. Forest hammered us 6-0 that night and I had been asked to report on the game for XTRA time, the Liverpool supporters' newspaper. I was required to produce 600 words on the match which, for somebody like me, who hadn't done anything like that before, was a daunting task. I was still in the process of moving my stuff from Boston to Liverpool at the time and, on the return journey, I stopped the van and went to the match. My mother came along with me and she actually picked the man of the match, which was quite difficult to do because Liverpool were absolutely awful that night. I bumped into Sammy Lee in the car-park before the game and with the forthcoming match report in mind, asked him how I should write it? He said, 'Basically, just write it as you see it!'

I know some people think we must be the footballing equivalent of trainspotters. To an extent, this is true, but saying that, we do get a lot of enjoyment from travelling to these games. And, the group of lads who I travel with are a really nice bunch. We've even got an Evertonian who comes to every Liverpool reserve game with us. He's a staunch blue, as well, but he gets a buzz from going to the match with us. There are a couple of guys among our number who are really competitive about the number of matches they attend each season. In previous years both of them have actually hit the 100 games mark, which is some feat. This included first team, reserves and A and B team matches. They're are times when you're sitting in a freezing cold, empty stand, at somewhere like Roker Park, and you do wonder, 'What the bloody 'ell am I doing here?' But you soon forget the cold wind and freezing rain when you arrive back at the car ready for the journey home to Liverpool. The result doesn't even matter that much, because, as I say, the buzz comes from just being there.

There is rarely any trouble at reserve games, though, for some reason, Leicester is always the exception to this rule. For some reason, they always have a mob in the main stand, looking out for anybody with a Liverpool shirt or scarf on. There was one particular instance when a gang of their boys chased a group of Liverpool supporters down the street after the reserve team game. The Liverpool fans they were chasing lived in Leicester anyway, but they still pursued them all around the ground. Another time was when Liverpool reserves played a pre-season friendly at Barrow. We were standing in their paddock and a couple of the local lads began snarling at us, shouting, 'Hey, you Scouse bastards, why don't you fuck off back to Liverpool?' But apart from those two incidents, I've never seen any trouble at the reserve team games. Saying that, I never really enjoy going to Goodison Park, either for first team or reserve team games, because their fans always seem to snarl at you for no reason.

I wouldn't like to estimate how much I spend on football each year. My season ticket for Anfield costs £250, for starters. With the cost of travel, both to first team and reserve away games as well as match tickets, food and travel expenses, it really is an expensive hobby, but an enjoyable one at that!

● ● ● ● ● ● ● ● ● ● ● ● ● ●

JOHN ALDRIDGE
Tranmere Rovers player/manager

Before I became a professional footballer I used to follow Liverpool all over the country along with my mates. I was brought up in Garston - 'under the bridge' - and used to attend New Heyes secondary school. My mates and I used to attend most of the away games involving the Reds. This was in the 1970's when you could guarantee every ground you vis ited would result in some kind of trouble - especially the London grounds. I used to hate going to the likes of West Ham and Chelsea because there would invariably be gangs of cockneys roaming the streets looking to attack the Liverpool fans. It never stopped me going, of course, because you just got used to that sort of thing, didn't you?

I never failed to get butterflies whenever the train pulled into Euston station because, being London, you never knew what to expect when you reached the station concourse or, indeed, the underground. You could guarantee there would always be a gang of supporters waiting to suss you out whenever Liverpool visited the capital. I think it's fair to say that you literally took your life in your hands at some of those away grounds, in those days.

And talking about London, it was in 1978 when Liverpool played Bruges in the European Cup final at Wembley that I saw the biggest away support ever. Liverpool must have had around 50,000 supporters inside the stadium that night. The atmosphere they created was unbelievable. The Bruges supporters were stuck at the top of the tunnel terraces - around 5,000 of them, all dressed in white. But they were literally surrounded on all sides by Liverpudlians. There was no trouble, of course. It was just one of those occasions when you knew Liverpool couldn't lose. When Liverpool paraded the cup after the game my mates and I were jumping up and down on the terraces in total joy. That was one of the best occasions I ever experienced following Liverpool. My mates and I had travelled down there in a mini-bus on the day of the game and afterwards we made sure there was plenty of ale on our bus for the journey back to Liverpool.

Another memorable game which I attended was the 1976 League title decider against Wolves at Molineux. We went on the ordinary train which left mid-afternoon from Lime Street. I've never seen so many Liverpudlians inside an away ground. It was unbelievable the amount of away support which had travelled from Merseyside. We were in the big Kop, behind one of the goals and the noise which was generated that night had to be heard to be believed. When Steve Kindon scored for Wolves in the first half the Liverpool supporters didn't let that setback bother them. They continued to shout for the team - my mates and I included. When we equalised it was sheer bedlam, all around the ground. And when we scored two late goals to seal the victory it was brilliant, with Liverpool supporters hugging each other in sheer joy.

When I made it as a professional footballer I had to stop going to watch Liverpool, obviously, but I still missed the camaraderie which my mates and I, along with all the other fans who travelled to the away games, used to muster. They were really good days then because everybody went to the away matches to have a good time. You would have a couple of beers before the game and then watch the match. Of course, Liverpool were winning everything at the time and this made it all the more enjoyable to watch.

The only time after that I saw Liverpool playing away from home was when I played for Newport County. It was the 1979/80 season and Newport had played on the Friday night - I can't remember who we played - but Liverpool were playing Bristol City at Ashton Gate the next day. I jumped on a train on Saturday morning and went to see them play. We won 3-1 that day with Ray Kennedy scoring one and Kenny Dalglish getting the other two goals.

CURTIS ROBB
Olympic Athlete

Unfortunately, due to both my commitments with both athletics and my college course I've been unable to get to either Anfield or any away grounds for the past couple of seasons. I'm currently based at Sheffield University where I'm in the middle of a five year medicine course. Saying that, whenever Liverpool play Sheffield Wednesday I always make a point of travelling over to Hillsborough to watch them in action.

Up till a couple of seasons ago I was a season ticket holder in the Kop at Anfield. I never missed a home game and was able to attend many of the away matches, too. I used to love travelling to all these away grounds because I would regard my attendance at these matches as another notch on my belt. It gave me pleasure to be able to say to friends, 'I've been to that ground.' I reckon most football supporters, no matter which team they support, would understand that statement.

Liverpool, by definition, would always take tremendous away support with them, wherever they played, be it in England or abroad. I don't know why but I always felt that Liverpool's away support was much more vociferous and passionate than it was at Anfield. Maybe I'm wrong but I feel there was always more enjoyment out of travelling to watch Liverpool play away from home. There was the romance of standing on the terraces of some away ground, knowing you were competing vocally with the home supporters. It was things like that which always gave me a real buzz. That's probably one of the reasons why the travelling support, of any team, is invariably young - be they male or female. I think the younger generation - the type who travel to most away games - have a lot more time on their hands and have less responsibility which obviously determines their attendance at these games.

Being involved in the Olympic games, which I was earlier this year, obviously hindered my attendance at Liverpool matches. That's something I've had to get used to over the last few years. But the merits of both Liverpool and indeed Everton is something which is discussed on many occasions, especially when my friend, Steve Smith, the Olympic high jumper is around. We have some tremendous discussions about the relative merits of both teams whenever we meet up. Steve is a rabid Evertonian and is even more biased than I am.

I remember being at Anfield with him a few seasons ago for a derby game. Steve had just had a number of stitches inserted for a head wound he had sustained while training. When Dave Watson scored for Everton in the Anfield Road end he jumped up to celebrate. A minute later Liverpool equalised and I jumped up in excitement, only to knock all his stitches out. There was blood everywhere. I tried to stem the flow coming from the side of his head, until the St. John's ambulance people arrived on the scene. We both laughed about the incident later but at the time it wasn't funny. And to rub salt into Steve's wound, Liverpool won the game 2-1.

● ● ● ● ● ● ● ● ● ● ● ● ● ●

IAN BROWN
Lift Engineer

Various away games in 1970's and 1980's

Scousers have always had a reputation for stealing. That stigma is probably quite justifiable, in my experience of travelling to see Liverpool play. We went to Old Trafford for a league game in the early 1980's and my brother, Stan, who was a scallywag of the highest order, came with us. Before the game I went into this sweet shop to buy ciggies. Our Stan accompanied me into the shop. The guy turned round to fetch the ciggies and as he handed them over I saw him looking over my shoulder. He suddenly shouted, 'hey, no.......stop!' I turned round and our Stan was running out of the shop with a crate of lemonade. Of all the fucking things you could have robbed.......our Stan had to rob a crate of lemonade! I walked out of the shop and our Stan was standing about ten yards away. The shopkeeper came out and confronted him. Stan picked up one of the bottles and waved it, saying, 'is it really worth it for a bottle of cream soda, mate?' The fella must have realised he was on a loser because he turned round and went back into his shop. The shopkeeper said, 'do you know him?' I replied, 'no, I've never seen him before in my life.'

* * * *

There was another time, again at Old Trafford, when my mates and I walked into this pub near to the ground, a couple of hours before the game. 'Two pints of lager and two pints of bitter, please mate,' one of the lads ordered. 'Sorry lads, no offence, but I can't serve you,' came the reply from the manager of the pub. We asked why and he said, 'see that space over there, by that wall?' We looked over and saw a big space where something had obviously been moved recently. 'What used to be there, lad?' I asked. 'Up till half an hour ago I had a fucking jukebox, there!' he replied. 'Four of your robbing Scouse bastards - sorry lads, no offence - came in, wheeled it out of the door and when I shouted what they were doing, they said, 'we're taking it to get mended, mate, you're alright!' The manager told us that five minutes later he'd walked to the end of the street to try and locate his jukebox only to find it on a piece of waste ground opposite. 'It was wrecked with not a fucking penny left in it,' he explained.

* * * *

I remember going to watch Liverpool play Sheffield Wednesday in a league game at Hillsborough a few seasons ago. I was thirsty and remember going into this shop to buy a can of coke. Next thing, the door burst open behind me and twenty lads stormed in and robbed the place blind.

They were like fucking ants. They left the place bare - they took everything. The fella behind the counter was shouting, 'what - the - fucking leave it - put that back!' I was standing there, waiting to get served. There wasn't a fucking ciggy left in the shop. Nothing in the freezer. Every bar of chocolate had disappeared. In fact, the place had been emptied. It was unbelievable. They had literally ransacked the shop. The fella sat down with his head in his hands, muttering to himself. His wife was stood in the corner crying her eyes out. So I said, 'have you got any coke left?' I felt last for asking but I didn't know what to say for the best.

✳ ✳ ✳ ✳

I know we're been talking about away games but I must mention this story from the 1960's concerning a game at Anfield. I can't remember who Liverpool were playing but my Uncle Freddie had gone to this game with his mate. Both of them used to knock off from the docks on Saturday dinner-hour and walk up to the ground. They used to stand near the front in the Anfield Road end and this particular game they were both stood there around ten to two, reading their programmes. My Uncle Freddie told us that he suddenly heard this swooshing noise. He turned to look up the terraces but couldn't see anything. Then he turned to look round and saw his mate lying on the floor with shit all over his face. Somebody had shit in a bag and threw it down the front of the terraces. His mate was lying on the floor vomiting because the smell was unbearable. It was in his mouth, in his ears, in his eyes, up his nose. The St. John's ambulance fellas ran over but nobody would go near him, because of the smell. Freddie's mate was shouting, 'help me, will you!' Eventually, they carted him out of the ground - though I don't know where they put him.

STEVEN MONAGHAN
Former road manager with The Farm

Evertonians, to this day, always skit Liverpudlians for the time we played West Ham at Upton Park, when supposedly only fourteen of us travelled to the game. This was a load of crap because there were around four hundred of us on the 'bright and early' train which left Lime Street at 6.25 that morning. The game itself was played around 1976 and I think Liverpool lost 2-0. We played Aston Villa the previous Wednesday night, at Villa Park, and had lost that one 5-1, so it wasn't a good week to be a Liverpudlian, I suppose.

West Ham was always a shady place to go to. As was the likes of Chelsea and Tottenham. But there was always a large number of Liverpool supporters who travelled to these games. I used to enjoy going to London because we would step off the train at Euston around 9 am and then a group of us would visit the shops in the West End. We would do our 'shopping' and then get something to eat before travelling onto the ground. You always had to watch your back in London because there were mobs of boys everywhere. You never knew who you would come up against. You might be travelling to Highbury on the underground and suddenly come across a mob of Chelsea, on their way to Crystal Palace, or something like that. Liverpool always took a good mob away from home and thankfully, were able to look after ourselves, most times. There were occasions when the opposition were a bit too strong for us, in terms of numbers, but everybody always seemed to make it back to Euston, safe and sound.

There was one particular game against QPR - I can't remember the score - but we'd had a good day out, anyway. Getting onto the train for the return journey a group of about twenty of us were walking through the carriages when one of the lads spotted Bill Shankly. 'Alright, Bill,' we all said in greeting. 'Hello, lads - been to the match?' he asked. It turned out he'd been helping to record an edition of This is your Life, for somebody. He asked us the score of the QPR v Liverpool game and eventually we got talking about football. You couldn't move in the carriage because all twenty of us were sitting transfixed as Bill began telling us tales of when he first started in football. It was brilliant listening to him. The journey home flew by and just as the train reached Edge Hill I asked if I could have a signed photo. Bill asked me to grab his bag from the rack and then he proceeded to sign a load of photographs of himself holding the FA Cup which we'd won in 1974. Unfortunately, my two mates, John Gargan and Joey Robinson lost out because there weren't enough photographs to go round. Bill Shankly replied, 'don't worry lads, you come round to my house tomorrow morning and I'll sign a photo for you.' Having gotten the former Liverpool manager's address from him, both John and Joey were really excited about the prospect of visiting his house.

The next morning both lads arrived around 11 am, just as Bill was manoeuvring his car out of the driveway. 'Bill, we've come for our photo's which you promised us last night, on the train,' the lads said in unison. 'Oh, I forgot all about that, lads,' he replied. 'Not to worry, come in.......Nessie, put the kettle on, I'll make these lads a cup of tea.' John and Joey couldn't believe it. Bill Shankly had postponed whatever he was doing just to welcome them into his house. The two of them sat on the edge of his couch, drinking tea and talking about football for a full hour. It turned out he was going to pick up his daughter to bring her back for Sunday lunch. The lads came out clutching their signed photographs and when we met up with them at the next home game they couldn't stop talking about their visit.

TONY CHINN
Former Chief Security Officer to Liverpool FC players and staff

How I got the job as Chief Security Officer for Liverpool Football Club is an interesting subject in itself. I was involved in teaching kids Shotokan karate in St. John's youth club in Dingle when Jack Ferguson, who was the director of the Holiday Inn hotel in Liverpool, came along to watch the kids in competitive action. He was impressed with the display our kids put on that night and as a consequence came over to talk. During the course of the conversation he mentioned there might be a job as security guard at the various Holiday Inn hotels which Liverpool FC used during away trips, both at home and abroad. I jumped at the opportunity and as a result found myself 'minding' the Liverpool players.

One of my first assignments was the 1984 European Cup final against AS Roma, in the eternal city. Liverpool were staying at the Holiday Inn by the Vatican and having secured the floor where the players and management were sleeping I was able to relax slightly. The only thing was, the hotel had been built to American standards which meant that there was a lift and stairwell on both ends of the corridor. This was fine if there turned out to be a fire but in terms of security it left a lot to be desired. Alongside ourselves was a small army of sub-machine gun wielding carabiniere, who placed themselves strategically in various parts of the corridor. The late Sir John Moores was also staying with the official party and he caused a slight scare when, in the middle of the night, he came out of his room and walked down the corridor. The Italian policemen were looking at him and probably wondering who this little old guy was. Sir John Moores was dressed in an old dressing gown and slippers and when he arrived at the end of the corridor he enquired as to the possibilities of acquiring some tea and toast. The carabiniere, on realising who he was, quickly sent somebody to fetch his late night supper.

Luckily, everything went smoothly that particular time but things weren't quite so easy on another occasion. The setting was the little town of Flint and the occasion was Ian Rush's wedding. Ian had asked me weeks earlier if I fancied the job and I'd replied that I certainly would consider it. Eventually, through Rushie's agent the deal was done and I set about employing various people to marshall the event. We anticipated there would be lots of people wanting to see the wedding but saying that, nobody could have envisaged just how many people there were around the church that day. It was unbelievable. There were hundreds of people lined up outside the church, all anxious to get a glimpse of Rushie and his bride, Tracy. To be honest, that wasn't the problem, though. We had been warned that the paparazzi (Italian press) would be trying anything to get inside the church to take photographs. Obviously, it was our job to stop them. This was just before Rushie signed for Juventus and that's a tale because the deal was that before he put pen to paper the Italian club wanted him married. Juventus had bought Rushie's mother one of those little Fiat Uno's to get herself around. I had to laugh because his mother is one of those little old ladies who is happy to go to the bingo with her mates. She is a brilliant old lady but, to be frank, she had no interest in the car. She's basically a working class, real down to earth type of person, like all of Rushie's family are. But those were the sort of things the Italians would do for you. Money was no object to them.

Anyway, back to the wedding and I'd picked thirteen men for the job. They were all Scousers, apart from one guy who was Iranian. The local press, on finding out about the job, arranged for a photo call on the grass at the back of the Holiday Inn in Paradise Street. So there we were, all dressed up in our black suits, white shirts and dickie bows. I must admit, we certainly looked the part. But the sting in the tail was that when the picture appeared in the papers the next day the caption read, 'Juventus send over twelve minders to guard Rushie!' That should have given us an idea of what was happening because come the day of the wedding the Italian press were trying every trick in the book to gain access to the church. Right opposite the church there was a block of maisonettes and the whole of the top balcony had been taken over by the paparazzi. They had obviously paid the residents to vacate the premises for the day. Earlier that day Rushie's agent had pulled me to one side and said, 'there's two journalists in particular I want you to watch out for,' he said. 'You'll know who they are when you see them. Whatever you do, don't let them in.' And he was right because as soon as I laid eyes on them I knew. Both were dressed immaculately. He wore a silk suit, with a long overcoat which was draped over his shoulder. His colleague, a woman of about thirty, was also dressed to kill. Both of them had deep tans and looked like what they were - top ranking Italian sports journalists. I warned the lads to keep an eye out for them, knowing they would be trying every trick in the book to get inside the church. I was standing at the entrance hall when they approached offering me five thousand pounds if I would let them into the church. I knocked them back, straightaway. It was all quiet for a few minutes until I walked around to the other side of the building and spotted the same pair talking to the priest, whose house was right next to the church. 'If you let us into your church my newspaper will buy a huge gold crucifix for your chapel,' the Italian was promising the little Irish priest. The latter was merely standing on his doorstep, listening to what the guy was saying. I stood close by but didn't intrude, at this stage. Thing was, I could see the priest folding up under the Italian's persuasive tongue. I had no doubts that his newspaper would have delivered the crucifix - or a Masserati - or even a holiday on some Mediterranean beach if only the priest would have allowed him into the church. After ten minutes of waving his arms and promising the earth I was certain the priest would let him inside. I said to myself, 'he's going to put me on the spot, here!' Next thing, the little Irish priest said to the Italian journalist, 'that sounds very good, sir, but I think you should confirm it with Mr. Chinn first.' That certainly put him in his place and we didn't see him or his female colleague after that.

Being a Liverpool supporter the job I had was a dream come true for me. Once I got past that initial point when the players accept you the job became brilliant. The biggest culture shock was realising that these lads go the toilet and sit in the same position as the rest of us. People put them on pedestals but really they are just like everybody else. They've got problems they have to deal with - they've got bad tempers - bad habits. The players then and now are just the same as us, really. It's just that the fans look up to them and it's a difficult responsibility to deal with. Look at John Barnes. He's Sophie, my eldest daughter's god-father and whenever he comes to our house in Dingle he makes a beeline for the fridge. To be honest, John would eat you out of house and home. He's a big eater - that's for sure!

I remember waking up one Sunday morning to the headlines in some rag which read, 'major expose - Liverpool FC minder blows the lid!!' I don't know where they got the story from but the next morning I went up to Melwood, looked the players in the eye and told them I hadn't spoken to any journalist and didn't know where this paper had gotten the story from. The players just laughed and told me not to worry about it. They knew I would never open my mouth. Not that there was anything to tell anyway.

The job varied in terms of tasks I had to do. Sometimes I would simply drive the players to various places, be they official functions or private trips. When Ian Rush moved to Juventus I travelled to Italy with him to help in that transitional period in his life. I was also employed to keep an eye out whenever the players or manager came into physical contact with the public; a book signing session in WH Smith's for example. Graeme Souness's new book, No Half Measures had just come out and Graham along with his ghost writer, Bob Harris were signing copies in the centre of Liverpool. The staff at WH Smith had built a podium which was situated to the right of the main entrance, as you walk inside. The place was packed out with fans and I had put two men on either side of the table, just in case somebody wanted to have a pop.

big guy - an Evertonian - started effing and blinding at Souey. The fella was drunk and he was having a real go at him. I wouldn't mind but there were women and kids in the queue and this fella wasn't about to stop his ranting and raving. Next thing, Souey started having a go back. Once he got started he really ripped the fella to bits. In the end, there was no need for us to get involved because the fella slunk out of the shop with loud cheers ringing in his ears from everybody in the shop.

I remember accompanying Rushie to a sports forum in a tobacco factory in Stafford. As soon as the audience were settled in their seats and Ian had taken his place on the podium this local radio sports commentator opened proceedings by mentioning Rushie's big nose. The audience went, 'oooh!' There was totally no need for things like that and the audience, to be fair, let their feelings be known on that score. Apart from that, the evening was a great success. In terms of my own position, it was little jobs like that which helped to further cement my relationship with the players and staff at Liverpool Football Club.

The job itself gave me a tremendous insight into the lifestyles of some rich and famous people, not just footballers. It was unbelievable the way they live their lives. Put it this way, it's so far removed from the way we live our lives that it's literally beyond comprehension - believe me. The money I earned was good - but not great. The real value came from the job I was doing and the places it took me to. I've been to Cyprus, Italy, Belgium, Scandinavia, all over Europe, in fact. I've made some good friends along the way, too. I'll tell you a little story before I finish. I run a youth project in Dingle which teaches local kids Shotokan Karate techniques. Like any organisation like ours we're always looking for funds to help in various activities such as day trips for the kids or a party at Christmas for them. Let me tell you that for the past three years our club have received a cheque for one thousands pounds from Liverpool Football Club Chairman David Moores. The man has given our club this money out of the goodness of his heart without any thoughts for gain for himself. Nobody, apart from the people involved with our club, know about this contribution, but I feel it's important to highlight such kind deeds.

THE VOICE OF ANFIELD

What The Players Say

STEVE McMANAMAN

I think the people who support Liverpool are among the finest, most loyal supporters in the world - I really mean that, too. We went to Finland for the European Cup Winners cup tie against My-pa 47 and before the game I went over to talk to some of the lads behind the goal. I knew a lot of them through seeing them at every away game. That's just it, you do get to know the people who come to support you. Not just at home but all over England and Europe. The game against the Finns is a good example of the great support Liverpool Football Club do receive because there was a large travelling away support at that game. And, you have to admire the very fact they turn up so many miles from home to watch us play.

Even the second leg of that tie summed up the loyalty of the Liverpool fans because there were 39,000 fans at Anfield that night to see a game that everybody presumed that we would win, anyway. Nevertheless, it was tremendous to see the ground so packed out for such a game. Before the match all the players thought we'd be playing in front of about twenty odd thousand supporters. To see almost 40,000 inside Anfield gave us a great lift because it showed how much the club means to the fans.

The Liverpool supporters have a long standing reputation for humour and they still possess a tremendous sense of fun, which is evident sometimes when we're playing. I'm a Scouser, anyway, and so I know where the fans are coming from when they're having a laugh at the match. I know a lot of the fans who come to the games personally and I know they would support the team through thick and thin. That's been proven over the years as Liverpool have never been short of support, whichever ground they've played on, both at home and abroad.

STAN COLLYMORE

Liverpool supporters are renowned the world over for their loyalty, support and passion for the game. Since I've been at the club I've had a few ups and downs but the fans have supported me right the way through. And, that's something I really appreciate. I think they are the best supporters in the country, both in terms of loyalty and support. I couldn't pay them a higher regard.

STIG INGE BJORNEBYE

To me, the Liverpool supporters are the best in the world - it's as simple as that! It's always a great experience to play in front of them - both at Anfield and at away grounds. The Liverpool supporters invariably turn out in droves to support the team, wherever the team are playing. This serves as a great spur to the players because, wherever we are playing, we know there will be Liverpool supporters making themselves heard inside the ground.

Before I came to Anfield I'd obviously heard of the Spion Kop but playing in front of it was a totally new experience for me. It was something I'd always dreamed about doing but never dreamed that one day I would play in front of the Liverpool fans. Even away from home the Liverpool supporters usually make themselves heard above the noise of the home fans. This gives the team a tremendous boost knowing the supporters have made the effort to come and watch you play. I know all the players appreciate the passion, loyalty and fanaticism which Liverpool supporters show both at Anfield and at away grounds all over the world.

LEE JONES

I know it's a cliché to say it, but I firmly believe that Liverpool supporters are, without doubt, the best in the world. As you know, playing in the Liverpool reserve side, I've known crowds of 10,000 or 12,000 for reserve games at Anfield. The recent game against a case in point because the crowd that night was huge compared to most other team's reserve crowds. Patrick Berger played that night and the response from the Liverpool public was tremendous. Playing in front of so many fans does have the effect of lifting your game - no doubts! You even get Liverpool fans turning up for away reserve games. You get to know the faces of the people who travel to these games. It could be a Thursday night in January but these people will still be there, sitting in the stand of some away ground, watching the team. I marvel at the loyalty and downright enthusiasm of these fans. It sure takes a lot of beating.

JASON McATEER

Liverpool supporters are very passionate about their football. I was brought up as a Liverpudlian anyway, and so I know what they're like. Obviously, they've been bred on success and so they know what the game is all about. We're top of the league at the moment and we seem to be doing really well. The players are hoping we can continue to give the Liverpool supporters something to cheer because they really do deserve the best we can give them. They've been turning up at Anfield in droves for many seasons now as well as at every away ground we play at. We really do appreciate the efforts the supporters make to come and watch us play.

The recent European Cup Winners cup tie against My-pa 47 was a good example of the support we've come to expect from the Liverpool fans because 39,000 turned out on a Thursday night to support us. The players appreciated the fact that so many fans had turned out to watch us play. It really brought home to us how much loyalty and passion the Liverpool supporters have for this club. Walking out onto the pitch that night we were surprised to see so many inside Anfield. It was certainly a tremendous fillip for all the players to see the ground so packed.

When we play away from home it's always the same. There are always plenty of Liverpool supporters occupying the away end of any ground, be it at home or abroad. They always make plenty of noise, too, which gives the players a great boost, knowing they'll never walk alone. The Liverpool fans are, and always have been, a very passionate set of supporters, which is good for the team because they will always cheer you on, no matter what is happening on the pitch. The players really do appreciate the support the Liverpool fans give to us.

JAMIE REDKNAPP

I think it's brilliant the way Liverpool fans support the team, not just in England but all over the world. They would support you through thick and thin. I've learnt that lesson from the very first day I arrived at Anfield. I've never known support like it. I think they are the best supporters in the world. Everywhere the team plays, be it Finland, Newcastle, London, they will be there, in their droves. It certainly gives the team a boost when we walk out for our pre-match kick-about to see so many Liverpool supporters filling up some away ground. It doesn't matter where we're playing - even pre-season friendlies - the fans will still turn out to watch us play. I marvel at the ingenuity of some of them because money is tight but they always find a way to get to the matches. They love their football and they love Liverpool Football Club - that's the top and bottom of it. The players really do appreciate the efforts they put in on our behalf, both to get to the games and for the support they give to us, both at Anfield and away from home.

JOHN BARNES

Over the past three or four seasons we haven't been able to deliver the goods on a consistent level for the fans and I feel that the Liverpool supporters are now getting their just rewards for the loyalty and support they've shown to us. It's still early days this season but I think the fans can appreciate that there could be exciting times ahead for the team.

Just to echo what some of the other players have said - I couldn't ever have envisaged such a huge crowd turning up to watch the game against the Finns. The game even had to be delayed to allow the fans into the ground. That's the kind of support the Liverpool players have become used to, over the years. Having stuck by us I firmly believe that this year will be the time when we finally reward them. And they deserve it. Having been used to so much success in the 1960's, 70's and 1980's they have had to endure a period in the doldrums in recent seasons. You could have half understood it if they had deserted us - but they haven't - they've stuck by us through thick and thin.

When I first came to Liverpool I likened the temperament of the people of this city to somewhere like Italy or South America. Scousers are not very 'English' in their attitudes. By that I mean they're not very reserved. They very much remind me of football supporters from Argentina or Naples - places like that - where the fans are very volatile and passionate about their football.

JOHN SCALES

The first thing which struck me when I first arrived at Anfield was the difference in crowd size. At Wimbledon our average gate was about 8,000 whereas at Liverpool the normal gate is around the 40,000 mark. Every time we walk out at Anfield to play I'm always amazed at the reception we receive from the Liverpool supporters. Since I came here the fans have been unbelievable in their support - both at Anfield and at every away ground we play at.

Coming to a big club like Liverpool it's normal to expect such support. Nonetheless, it still amazes me how vociferous and passionate the fans are. They turn up, week in week out, both home and away, and you cannot help but be impressed by how much support a club like Liverpool receive from their fans - it's phenomenal!

The Liverpool supporters are certainly the most educated and sporting fans I've ever come across. They know their football so well that you can sometimes feel tension within yourself, knowing that the fans literally live and breathe their football. At times it's almost as if they're out there playing the game with us. There's such a close affinity that exists between both Liverpool players and supporters that you feel as one when you're playing sometimes.

Liverpool supporters have seen so many great players wear the red shirt down the years that it's almost an education playing in front of them. They know what's going on and understand what they are watching. I certainly enjoy playing in front of the Liverpool fans.

ROBBIE FOWLER

Ever since I came into the side I've been brought up on the passion and excitement which Liverpool supporters continually generate at matches. The noise inside Anfield is phenomenal, at times and this has the effect of lifting my game. Even playing away from home the Liverpudlians always make a lot of noise - often out-shouting the home supporters. It's always nice to know that wherever the team are playing there will be plenty of Liverpool fans inside the ground, cheering us on. I know the other players appreciate the efforts which go into following us all over the country and abroad.

Without the fans alongside us we would struggle at times. That's why it's so good to know that we can count on them for support when the going gets tough, which it does at times. Full marks to the Liverpool fans - both at Anfield and away from home because, to me, they are among the best supporters in the world.